# Self-Compassion Workbook

How to accept yourself

Sadie Quail

Copyright 2021 – Sadie Quail

# GET THE AUDIOBOOK VERSION
## of "Self Compassion Workbook"
# FOR FREE WITH A 30 DAY AUDIBLE TRIAL

Following this link for USA :

https://www.audible.com/pd/B0933NFF4M/?source_code=AUDFPWS0223189MWT-BK-ACX0-252040&ref=acx_bty_BK_ACX0_252040_rh_us

Following this link for UK:

https://www.audible.co.uk/pd/B0934M3D9G/?source_code=AUKFrDlWS02231890H6-BK-ACX0-252040&ref=acx_bty_BK_ACX0_252040_rh_uk

---

I'd be really happy if you could leave a **short feedback** on Amazon, it means a lot to me! Thank you

https://www.amazon.com/Self-Compassion-Workbook-accept-yourself-ebook/dp/B08XMFBXK7

Would you like to download a _free_ Pdf about the Yin and Yang in the Self-Compassion? **Click or follow the link:**
https://forms.aweber.com/form/99/1144718499.htm

# Table of Contents:

Introduction     8

Chapter 1: The first step – Letting letting go the past and why?
    9

Chapter 2: Responsibility – how to change your trajectory?     21

Chapter 3: Awareness and Mindfulness - How to set realistic expectations and how to meet them?     32

Chapter 4: Setting goals in the right place–valuing your happiness, changing the way you speak to others and yourself     49

Chapter 5: Self Image - Recognizing that the only thing you can control is yourself and letting go of self-criticism     62

Chapter 6: Daily practices – stress response, how to eliminate negative energy and care for yourself     74

Chapter 7: Daily practices – meditation techniques and breathing exercises, to start and end the day for better sleep     91

Chapter 8: Daily practices – virtues and utilizing your surrounding     108

Chapter 9: Road mapping – finding motivation in yourself     129

Chapter 10: Importance of self confidence – letting go of the Codependency 143

Chapter 11: Everything you need to know about Codependency 165

Chapter 12: A guide to forming healthy relationships 186

Conclusion 204

# Introduction

Congratulations on purchasing *Self-Compassion Workbook*, and thank you for doing so. Does your inner critic refrain you from achieving your full potential? Are you stuck in the toxic cycle of perfectionism? Then you are at the right place because what you need is a new mindset – a mindset that will allow you to practice self-compassion. In every phase of life, you will face some inner obstacles like insecurity, sadness, and anxiety, and in order to overcome these, you have to walk on the path of self-compassion. In this book, I will teach you how you can do that and love yourself. After reading this book, you will be able to cultivate kindness, break the loop of self-criticism, and embrace yourself for the person you are. Practicing self-compassion is not that hard. There are a range of things that you can do, meditation and breathing practices that you can engage in to cultivate self-compassion, and all of that will be discussed in this book. There comes a time in all our lives where we face burnout. The important thing to do is not to ignore that burnout and take the right measures. Instead of beating yourself up for small mistakes, you need to find a way to motivate yourself.

Mental health is a complex space and there is no need to hurry. You have to find an approach that is sustainable and effective. In this book, I have suggested numerous measures that you can take to change your mindset and walk on the path of self-compassion. Now, you must be thinking – what will self-compassion give you? Well, it will give you a lot of things, but most importantly, it will allow you to be you, and you will start seeing the world in a different way. You will no longer be bothered by what others think of you. At first, you might be skeptical of the idea of self-compassion. Trust me; I have been there. But keep following everything mentioned in this book, and once you see the results, you will start believing. The real beauty of self-compassion lies in the fact that it gives more importance to your mental health and well-being over perfectionism. There are plenty of books on this subject on the market, thanks again for choosing this one! Every effort was made to ensure it is full of as much useful information as possible, please enjoy! Make sure to leave an honest feedback on Amazon if you enjoy, I'd really love to read your thoughts about it.

# Chapter 1:

# The first step –

# Letting go of the past and why?

In a lot of situations, our past experiences stand between us and our future selves- without us even realizing this actively- and greatly shape the ways in which we negotiate throughout our lives. Most of us bring with ourselves a great deal of emotional baggage and unresolved issues from the past which, even if we think we have let go of, are buried somewhere at the back of our minds and impact our decision-making skills in several direct and indirect ways. Therefore, in order to understand our own selves better, and to actually practice the act of self-compassion or being kind to ourselves, it is really important that we learn to let go of our pasts, especially in cases when it is boggling our present and future selves down in one way or the other.

**Why should we let go of our past?**

At one point in our lives, we actively need to let go of the past- our past failures, past expectations, past hopes, dreams, and the hurt all of it have been causing us. When someone holds on to their past, it means that they are allowing fear to take over them. This fear is the fear of rejection and the fear of loss. On one side, we are scared to lose the ways in which we had felt in the past- as we also feel that in a way, these feelings have come to shape as we are now- not realizing that there is little merit in holding on to feelings which cause us pain and unhappiness. On the other, we are also scared of the rejection we believe our present or future self could face, based on the experiences we have had in the past around rejection. However, we really need to understand that it is integral for our growth that we should give ourselves some space to breathe, some space to reinvent ourselves and see ourselves in a positive light as if we keep dwelling in our past experiences of rejection, we deny ourselves any scope of development. We need to begin this process with the understanding that *letting go* is not the same as *giving up*. Just because you are choosing not to delve into things that happened to you at some capacity in the past does not- in any sense- mean that you are disregarding or giving up on your own experiences and lived reality. It just means that instead of holding on to these past experiences which are weighing you down, you are actively choosing to adopt a much healthier outlook towards things. Your past would always still be there for you to get back to;

however, it is not something you can change, no matter how hard you try to. On the other hand, your future is probably the only aspect of your life which you can mold out to be in a way you want it to be, which makes it the natural decision to prioritize over your past.

**How to let go of our past?**
Having said enough about the importance of why we should let go of our past, I will now discuss how realistic the process actually is and how we can really try and dissociate ourselves from our past identities and experiences. Although this might sound much easier said than done, listed below are a few ways in which we could try to let go of the past.

**Treat yourself with kindness:** Often, we are so focused on expressing kindness towards the other people in our lives, we actually forget to stop for a minute and reassess how kindly we are treating our own selves. It is of utmost importance that we treat ourselves with as much kindness as we could possibly spare, if not even more. This might include saying kinder things about ourselves and cutting down on self-deprecation and self-hate, thinking about ourselves in a more positive light, writing down daily positive affirmations as a form of journaling so that we are constantly reminded of the endless possibilities we hold within ourselves. It is really important to realize that if we are not treating ourselves with kindness and compassion, then we cannot possibly continue to treat other people the same, because we would be draining ourselves of a lot of positive, inspiring emotions without allowing to replenish them through different ways of practicing self-love and compassion.

**Try and be less judgmental about the world around you:** One of the ways in which we can let go of our past and try and begin practicing self-compassion is by starting to be less judgemental about the world around us. Although it is true that some of the assumptions and judgments we make are based on some truth, they still do not take into account how unpredictable our lives actually are and how little we know on the surface about what other people are going through in their lives. If we are not allowing others to make mistakes and explore new possibilities, it will be very hard to do that towards our own selves. Besides that, having assumptions about other people also constantly inhibit us because assumptions do not allow us to completely take in what other people- and our interactions with them- have to offer, as we are always blinded by our judgments about them. A lot of these assumptions are also related to how we have been treated by people in the past, and often, we use judgments as a protective measure, which is all the more reason for us to let go of constant judgments and assumptions about the people we let into our lives.

**Forgive the mistakes you have made:** This one almost goes without saying, but we cannot really let go of our past if we do not start to let ourselves make mistakes. Once we acknowledge the fact that we have made quite a few mistakes in our past, we can begin to accept our mistakes and love ourselves in spite of them. One of the biggest reasons why we find it so hard to let go of our past is because we tend to hold onto bitter memories more strongly than we hold on to more positive ones, and a lot of these memories naturally would revolve around some mistake we had made- knowingly or otherwise. This is why we constantly shift a lot of blame to ourselves, which leads us to set lower expectations from ourselves in the future as well. Forgiving the mistakes we have made in the past does not just help us have a more balanced outlook towards the lives we are leading currently but also sets us up for a future with more promises and possibilities.

**Prioritize physical and mental self-care:** I cannot stress how important it is to practice self-care, and by self-care, I mean care that extends to both our minds and bodies. Although a lot of self-help books and pages would have us believe that self-care only has to do with bubble baths and shopping trips, it is incredibly crucial to realize that self-care does not necessarily always have to be indulgent. Of course, we deserve to buy ourselves a treat from time to time as well as the luxury of a long bubble bath, but a lot of times, really taking care of ourselves means investing in a lot of trivial and mundane tasks which have a better payoff in the longer run. Self-care means cutting toxic people and associations from the past of our lives and letting ourselves grow beyond the restrictions our past selves have set for us. It also means allowing us to make better decisions than we had in the past in terms of what we really mean by *care-* in the past, we might not have been consistent about self-care, which is why our present selves might be a little wary about the premise, but a part of self-care is allowing ourselves to start afresh and redefine what care means for us and how do we want to practice it in our own lives. Other than that, making more compassionate and conscious choices that have the potential to drastically change our lives and the way in which we see it is incredibly effective when it comes to mental self-care.

**Shift the focus from yourself:** The past holds us back also because a lot of it has to do with our own thoughts, processes, and actions- at least in our minds. This is why we also tend to fixate on a lot of smaller things from the past and tend to place the blame for nearly everything that had gone wrong on our own shoulders. This happens not because it is actually true, but because we think so long and hard about the things *we* had done in the past that after one point, it becomes simply instinctive to link everything with our own actions. However, what really helps in such a situation is shifting the focus from ourselves and look at the larger picture- including the role others have played in the things which have come to shape the turn our lives have taken in the longer run. The larger picture also serves as a helpful guide to the much-needed realization that, in many cases, we tend to assign more importance to our actions, whereas in reality, they might be completely unrelated to the consequences we hold ourselves to be accountable for.

**Try to find your passion:** In a lot of cases, it is difficult to let go of our past because of the associations we have made with it in terms of our actions. One way to start fresh, with a blank slate, is to take some time out for ourselves and spend some time introspecting about what really moves us and where do our passions lie. In a way, this will help us rediscover ourselves, which is a very certain way to break many of the associations we have made with the past and which continue to weigh us down.

**Invest in the things you enjoy doing:** Once we have figured our passion out, it is also very important that we do not leave it at that and actually invest in the things, hobbies, and activities we really enjoy doing. Whether it means to sign up for a new class, read a new book, or starting a small business, it is always worth the time and effort to actively invest in our passions. Once we invest in the things we enjoy doing, we are on our way towards a future which we can mark using these passions and not using the hurt and unpleasantness we have come to carry forward from our past lives for a very long time.

**Change your overall mindset:** This one is probably the vaguest but the most important item on this list. It also quite neatly sums up almost all the other points, turning them into a larger actionable goal. Changing our overall mindset and adopting a more positive and realistic one can do absolute wonders in the way we look at our lives and the trajectory they have taken through time and space- which also means that a new mindset might be one of the easiest ways in which we could undo a lot of linkages we continue to make with what happened to us in the past. Adopting a mindset that makes us more accepting- to our mistakes and to the possibilities the future has in store for us- is perhaps one of the more lasting and harder ways of practicing self-care. To sum up, this chapter went over how learning to let go of our past is an essential step towards practicing how to be more compassionate to own selves. It also quickly glossed over why it is actually important and necessary in letting go of the past and everything in it, which is hindering our self-growth, ending with a list of actionable items through which you could actually achieve that.

# Chapter 2:

# Responsibility –

# How to change your trajectory?

When we are talking about the idea of self-compassion and how to ideally chart a way out to achieve it, we need to keep in mind that the way is filled with a few obstacles on the course. One of such obstacles will be discussed in this chapter. While trying to understand and practice self-compassion, we need to assume responsibility for certain things, thoughts, and actions on our part so that we can acknowledge what we have done and then work from there- in an informed way- ahead. Several self-help tips would suggest you blindly forget the past and plunge into planning a better future, but such short-sightedness, especially if you are practicing it deliberately, is bound to do more harm than good. We cannot simply erase all that has happened in the past. Neither do we need to fixate on it. Once we assume complete responsibility, it becomes easier for us to pick up the lessons we want to carry ahead in our lives; this also helps us to identify our flaws better- which is the first step in trying to fix them.

**What does it mean to assume responsibility?**
In order to be more compassionate to our own selves, we need to take responsibility for not just our past actions

but also for our future. Now, the first question that might pop into your head after reading this is what does it *actually* means to take responsibility. It is good to approach this discussion in a way that introduces you to two options. You can either believe that life happens *to* you, or you can believe that life happens *for* you. How you see life- and the role you play in it- goes a long way in determining how active or passive you are (or can be) when it comes to assuming self-responsibility.

If you merely believe that life is something that is happening to you, then the stance you are automatically assuming is very passive in nature. It implies that good or bad, the events you are facing are sort of inevitable, and you have no other option than to accept them and try and deal with their consequences. On the contrary, if you are more actively analyzing your life events, then you would be of the opinion that you have a very integral role to play in shaping the path these events take. This way, you are bound to assume responsibility for your own life instead of meekly giving in to the worldview that you would take things simply as they come. Once you start taking responsibility for your life, once you start believing that you actually have a role to play in charting out things that happen to you in life, then you would be gradually working towards bringing a real change in your life. Now, this change could be good or bad, depending on the circumstances, but the positive thing is that it would at least be driven by the actions you have chosen to take, which is in itself way better than being a silent spectator about the things which hold the potential of having a great impact on you.

**How to actively take responsibility?**

These are some easily achievable ways in which you can be more aware and active while taking responsibilities in your day-to-day life:

**Shift the blame from other people:** Placing the blame on other people is one of the quickest and easiest ways to get out of a tricky situation. It guarantees you escapism but also does not take you very far. Even if you do not own up about your actions in front of other people, there is no way that you could lie to yourself regarding something which you should have taken responsibility for, ideally. Blaming other people is a rather cowardly thing to do in many instances because it allows us to live in denial, and denial usually does not do much good. Once we shift the blame from other people and try and see how we could have behaved differently in certain situations and how different the outcomes could then have been, it might be a lot easier to mend our mistakes. These would then also serve as lessons for how to act (or not) in the future. On the other hand, once we place the blame on someone else's shoulders, we have no way of making sure how they would react to the situation and how they would try and fix something that affected not just them but also you. If the responsibility lies on you, then only you are in charge of taking action- in the situation and also in your life in general. This is exactly why shifting the blame from other people is a healthy practice, as it really trains us on how to be more involved, accountable, and actionable in our own lives.

**Allow yourself some mistakes:** It is a given that none of us are above all mistakes. We are not perfect, and expecting ourselves to be perfect would only result in a travesty. The expectation of perfection brings with itself a lot of unnecessary pressure. Therefore, it is also very important that, at times, we are able to simply let go and allow ourselves to make some mistakes in the process. When I say this, I, of course, do not mean that these mistakes are potentially life-altering in terms of their consequences (if they are, they are NOT the mistakes worth making, obviously); I just mean that these are trivial enough to not stress too much about. Apart from this, making mistakes is also sometimes a very good reality check for a lot of people, as it can possibly bring about a change in the way in which they see and approach things. A mistake might be the much-needed reset button for a lot of people, which is why it is absolutely alright- and perhaps even necessary- to have your guards down at times and to make yourself open to errors. However, it is also important to acknowledge these errors and not have other people pick up your pieces (as has been discussed in the previous point). It is also important to not let these allowance make way for unnecessary excuses, which we are going to discuss next.

**Excuses won't take you too far:** Excuses are very dangerous traps that we often build for our own selves. Sure, they work most of the time and are bound to work, too, but they also make us extremely complacent and trick us into finding the easy way out at times when we really do not have to. When we allow our faults to be covered by the excuses we come up with, we are not letting ourselves learn from the mistakes we are making. This would only mean that the next time around, we are going to make the same mistake once again because we are subconsciously aware that it is possible to easily get away with it. There are ugly parts about ourselves which we need to face if we are trying to assume responsibility in our own lives, and excuses only shut up the channels of negativity more and more to the point that we are completely oblivious about the flaws which had us making these excuses up in the first place. Excuses also often lead to us playing the victim card, and if dragged out for too long, this might result in a loss of credibility, especially when there are other people involved to whom we owe some accountability. And it is obvious that there is absolutely no way to grow when there is no personal accountability. It is not being denied that many a time, excuses are absolutely genuine and are very much needed, but overutilizing excuses as simply a means of getting away with things and not turning up when required sets a bad precedent, prevents our growth, and also in a way, make us live a dishonest life.

**Be mindful about the impact others have on you:** Blaming other people and relying on excuses as a crutch can often lead us to believe that we are the victim in every situation in our lives. If this is the way we are feeling, then it might be a good idea to take a step back and look at the larger picture at hand- are we really a 'victim,' or are we not aware of the ways in which different situations and people impact us? If we see two people gossiping in the corner of the room, it is really up to us to decide if their remarks are generic or whether they are directed towards us in particular. If we do not know the contents of what these two people are talking about, how we assess the impact of this situation has a huge role to play in how we see ourselves- as a 'victim' or otherwise. If we change the way we look at certain things and react to certain situations, then high chances are that we can bring about a change in the degree to which we let other people have an effect on us. This is where it might be useful to know about a psychological term known as the locus of control. Some people have an internal locus of control, whereas others have an external one. Depending on our locus of control, we react to situations. If we have an internal locus of control, we are much more likely to hold ourselves responsible for things that impact us; in the case of an external locus of control, we are more likely to place the responsibility on external factors (including other people). This is why it is easier for some people to automatically assume responsibilities, while it is a little harder for others. It is an absolutely natural thing and does not indicate any inherent 'strength' or 'weakness' in a person that cannot be worked on. Once we are aware of how our thought processes work, it is not impossible to change our perspectives and take responsibility.

## Why should we take responsibility for our lives?

After the *what* and the *how* we come to the most crucial point- the *why* of taking responsibilities. This boils down to the same old cliche- you are responsible for your own life and your own happiness. We should take responsibility for our own lives, in our own lives, simply due to the fact that we cannot wait around for a fairy godmother to step in and solve all our problems at our own convenience. While it is true that a lot of us are brought up in very protected and comfortable environments where we never really had to face the dilemma of taking our own responsibilities or 'being on our own,' it is also true that these bubbles of comfort are always temporary. The moment we are compelled to step out into the world, we are instantly faced with decisions and responsibilities we have to assume. These might not be grand things but can be many tiny things that eventually add up to larger ways of living our lives. The best way to make sure that we are living our lives on our own terms is to not rely on anyone else to make our lives easier and try and do it ourselves. It is not possible to achieve all that we aspire for at the very first go, and it really is alright to achieve in bits and parts, as that would help us learn how to process further from that point, instead of having the option of falling back on a safety net. At the end of the day, we need to keep in mind that two steps forward and one step backward still amount to one step forward, and as long as our steps forward are being prompted by ourselves, we are on the right way ahead in our lives.

# Chapter 3:

# Awareness and Mindfulness –

# How to set realistic expectations and how to meet them?

Before we discuss in detail how and why we need to set realistic expectations, it might be helpful to take a look at the concept of mindful self-compassion.

**What is meant by mindful self-compassion?**

Since we have already been discussing self-compassion in a few of chapters in this book so far, it might be time to shift our focus to more specific ways in which we could understand and practice being compassionate to ourselves. Mindful self-compassion is a way of practicing compassion through which we could not just get to understand our own self a lot better, but can also help us set boundaries better and interact more fruitfully with the people around us. However, like many self-care practices, mindful self-compassion is not something that comes naturally to us. It is a little tricky to start with and definitely needs a lot of work on our part to keep at it, but at the same time, it also has a great payoff. Mindfulness has been defined by the American Psychological Association as "A moment-to-moment awareness of one's experience without judgment. In this sense, mindfulness is a state and not a trait. While it might be promoted by certain practices or activities, such as meditation, it is not equivalent to or synonymous with them" (APA, 2012). What this definition, combined with our understanding of self-compassion, means is that in order to practice mindful self-compassion, we need to be really *present* and *aware* of the ways in which we develop emotional support for ourselves in a better way, equipping us to be kinder towards ourselves. There have been many academic studies that have attempted to find and establish a connection between mindfulness and self-compassion. These studies have led the research, in general, to be targeted towards not just the connection between these two ideas but also on the many ways in which one could actually practice mindful self-compassion in their own life. In order to be more mindful about how/if you are compassionate to yourself, it might help to start with asking yourself what are the things which are holding you back from being kinder to yourself in the very first place. This can be achieved by focusing on the negative self-beliefs which you harbor within yourself, and these beliefs can be explored in many ways, one of which being facing yourself with some prompts which you must directly answer.

These prompts can include the following:

- How does it (the negative self-belief) make you feel once written down?
- When did you first develop this belief? What experiences are connected to it?
- What external experiences or situations trigger this belief about yourself?
- Who encourages this belief about yourself?
- How would your life look if you didn't believe this about yourself?

Once you have confronted these negative ideas you had about yourself, you can continue your exploration of mindful self-compassion by taking various steps such as explore various thoughts and emotions (especially positive ones or ones you did not actively allow yourself to experience earlier), developing awareness about your possible triggers, and learning to stop living in denial of things and confronting things you have tried to avoid for a longer time. All of these would help you be more mindful about your needs in general, which would help you understand your capacities and limits. Without first exploring your limits, it might be redundant to discuss how to set expectations from yourself because a lot of goal setting mostly revolves around the practice of being able to set healthy boundaries and being able to say 'no' to things that you either do not want (to do) or cannot possibly commit to.

**How do we actually set realistic expectations?**

We need to keep in mind that any expectation we set involves some commitment we make to other people, in one way or the other. Even in the case of the expectations in terms of self-progress, our actions still end on having some degree of impact on the people around us. Therefore, it is good to be mindful while setting expectations since the outcomes of these expectations almost often affect other people. Once we are aware of these consequences, we can use them as a motivating factor for setting expectations and making commitments that are simply more realistic and attainable.

Here are a few ways in which we can actually set realistic expectations:

**Be aware of your limit**: We are only human and can only take up so much on our plates at a time. However, a lot of the time, we do tend to overestimate our capacities and take up a lot more than we can actually deliver on. There might be a lot of reasons behind this, one the most obvious ones being that a lot of us do have a serious problem is saying 'no' to other people. It can also be very true that we are just intrigued about a lot of things and therefore are interested in dipping our toes into one too many passion projects. However, we need to be very mindful of our limits while we make any commitments or set any expectations up for ourselves. It is also important to remember that our limits vary from time to time and are based on a lot of external circumstances. We might be able to commit 10 hours per week to a volunteering project during certain months of the year when the workload is not that high, but during the busier months, we might be only able to set apart 4-5 hours for the same job, regardless of how dedicated we are to it. This is exactly why we need to not just be aware of our limits but also of how they tend to fluctuate depending on other factors. Being able to predict how much we can take on our plates a little beforehand is a really useful skill and is very helpful in terms of setting realistic expectations.

**Decide on flexible deadlines:** Depending on the tasks we are undertaking and the goals we have set for ourselves, we must allow ourselves to be flexible, especially in terms of the deadline that you are working towards. Flexible deadlines help break the monotony as well as keep you interested in the task at hand. However, it is true that not everything we take up would essentially have a flexible deadline. For example, if you are working on a freelancing project, you can easily ditch the 9 to 5 grind and set up flexible deadlines and work hours for yourself, but if you are working on a college project, that might not allow you the same degree of flexibility. But what you can do in this case is set up different deadlines and smaller goals for yourself so that you can break the project up into parts and work your way around instead of chasing one larger, intimidating deadline. Flexible deadlines also have their cons (they can easily lead to procrastination), so keep that in mind as well, and make sure they are not outweighing the pros in terms of the independence we get while working with them.

**Hold yourself back from over-committing:** This one goes sort of hand-in-hand with the first point on this list, but it cannot be ever stressed enough that over-committing to tasks can be extremely draining for us. It will also invariably lead to us delivering stuff while we are compromising on its quality, which is a lot worse than taking up only as much as we can chew but doing those tasks as best as we can. Committing to too many things is one of the more surefire ways of leading ourselves into a physical and mental state of burnout, which is really hard to come back from. In case there are simply a lot of things we need to take up, and we absolutely cannot avoid committing to any of those, it helps to manage our time more smartly and make sure that in spite of the multiple projects we have taken up, their deadlines are not coinciding. This way, we can channel different amounts of energy to different projects depending on the urgency they come along with.

**Set up a proper line of communication:** This one is especially important if the expectations you have set up involves another person, for example, if you are reporting to someone or are working alongside another person. In cases like these, it is absolutely significant to set up a proper line of communication with anyone else you are accountable to because that would automatically do away with a lot of possible miscommunication or misunderstandings that might take place during the course of your time working together. Once a proper channel of communication has been set up, it would also be really essential to set up some trust so that you can communicate your problems, requirements, and other expectations from the work that is being done overall without much inhibition. A proper line of communication is also important so that if you are facing any difficulties with work, you have someone to turn to and seek advice from, which would prevent things from becoming a lot tougher otherwise.

**Check what is holding you back:** What also happens in a lot of cases that there might be some baggage- from the past or otherwise- which is holding back or is influencing your decisions greatly in terms of the expectations you are setting from yourself. What often happens is that we idealize a 'perfect' outcome in our heads, which is why we either do not commit enough to something or we over-commit to things out of the belief that we are not doing enough to prove our productivity. For either of these cases, what is holding us back from setting realistic expectations is not exactly our work ethics, but are other external factors that need some self-introspection in the first place to be addressed in an adequate way. Therefore, it might be a very good idea to try to address our shortcomings in terms of setting expectations and assess them, keeping the large picture in mind and not just the current task at hand.

**Use positive affirmations:** This is one of the more long-term things we can work with. Using positive affirmations is a way to restore our faith in ourselves as well as keeping us firmly grounded, which eventually serves as a stepping stone for us to understand ourselves better and make better decisions when it comes to setting any expectations. The positive affirmations can be in the form of gratitude journaling, can be done through several self-care apps and software, or can even just be a sticky note on which you jot down reminders for yourself to stay grounded without getting overwhelmed about all the things going around you. There are several journaling prompts which you could find online, which can be very helpful when it comes to finding positive affirmations that work for you and will help you make the most out of them. Although this one sure looks like a stretch with regards to how little it promises on actionability in comparison with the other items on the list, this one is great with resetting our mindsets and just the way in which we perceive expectations and commitment in general, which is one of the key steps in practicing mindful self-compassion.

**How can we meet the expectations we end up setting?**

Now that we have (sort of) sorted out how to set realistic expectations, we also need to talk about the *doing* bit, about how we meet the expectations which we have set, because, let's be real, at the end of the day, any thought without action is simply not worth investing in. Also, it is absolutely alright to feel overwhelmed with the expectations we have set, but figuring out a system that works for us can actually do wonders for how we go about working towards them. For some people, a project-based long term system works out the best, while for

others, shorter, goal-based techniques work better, and completely different things might be helpful for other people. So, don't be afraid to try different things out until you can place your finger on one which is apt for you! In case you are still a little confused (which is again, alright!) about how to actually practice meeting your expectations, the items listed below might be of some help:

**Have a clear understanding of deliverables:** A deliverable is simply something- tangible or otherwise- that we are expected to produce or achieve as the end goal of any expectation we set for ourselves, be it for the long run or the short. One of the most important ways of meeting our expectations is to have great clarity about what is expected at the end of it. In case we are unsure of what we are supposed to deliver, things can go wrong in many ways- we might overwork or underwork ourselves, or we might even produce something which was not required in the first place, which will have us devote even more time and energy in fixing that later. Do not be afraid of asking follow-up questions and clarifications- as many as it takes for you- to be absolutely sure about the deliverables so that you are not working in the dark in order to meet the expectations.

**Remember to always write it down:** This might sound like a reminder from your primary school teacher, but it genuinely does help out very, very much to write down things such as deadlines, deliverables, specific goals, aims and objectives, and so on. This could be done digitally, in a planner, or even on a random piece of paper (in case you are resorting to this, make sure to be careful about not losing the piece), but having your goals set out in front of you *visually* does help a lot. There has also been a great deal of psychological research which had shown how it is easier for many people to break down larger projects in their head when visualization tools were made available to them. Writing things down simply helps you keep track of it, which in turn helps you get it done because there is little to no chance that you will forget something which you have taken the effort to document this way.

**Try and be transparent at all times:** In case you are facing any problems, be transparent and honest about them. In case you are working on something which does not seem to be worth your time midway through the project, be honest about it and seek advice from other people. Even if the expectation you have set for yourself is a little easier with reference to your standard of work and you want some extra work, try and be honest about it. No, that would not make you desperate; it would just give everyone (and especially, your own self) a very good idea about what you can and cannot grapple with, which will make it easier to set and meet expectations in the future. Transparency is a really crucial thing to practice in order to be more compassionate to yourself as it ensures that you are genuine about your own needs and boundaries.

**Make sure to get feedback:** Asking for feedback might sound a little apprehending, but it is, in fact, quite the opposite. Feedback will only help you improve yourself and your work, and it is also very helpful if you are open to receiving constructive criticism and feedback as it will help you figure out if you are setting very realistic expectations or not. It might seem like a good idea to finish a submission and leave things as it is because 'nothing can be really be changed once the thing is done,' but it is also true that that is not the last thing that would need to be done by you, and there always will be the next time. Therefore, treating any feedback not as criticism for your *last* assignment but as pointers before the beginning of your *next* assignment is a much better and more positive way of looking at it and using it to your benefit.

**Decide if this is an expectation worth setting:** Last but not least, as we have discussed previously in this chapter, sometimes we take up things just for the sake of it and end up spending a huge chunk of our time and energy tackling it. However, our efforts might be better preserved than spent on things which we are not really dedicated to. Therefore, it is a very useful practice to introspect, weigh out the pros and cons, and ask ourselves the crucial question- *is this an expectation really worth setting up for myself?* The answer would be no for more things than you can perhaps imagine. Just think of all the energy we would be saving up if we can allow ourselves to be a little critical of our commitments. This energy would then be used better- invested in something we are actually passionate about, or even saved up for the time we might need it more than now. Again, quitting on certain things does not mean giving up. In many cases, it just means that we are training ourselves to make better and more informed choices, which is essential for our growth.

To sum up, in this chapter, we first went over the concept and process of mindful self-compassion. Next, we discussed the different ways in which we can set realistic expectations for ourselves are, and finally, we took a glance at some actionable items which can greatly help us in assessing and meeting the expectations we are setting up.

# Chapter 4:

# Setting goals in the right place – Valuing your happiness, changing the way you speak to others and yourself

Now that we have already discussed how to set and meet realistic goals for yourselves, the next step towards being more self-compassionate deals with learning how to value your happiness through changing the way you speak to both others as well as your own self. The main question which arises out of this step is whether there is any relationship between compassion and self-compassion or not. In other words, does being kinder to other people help you be kinder to yourself (or the other way round)?

A very common saying out of many self-help manuals states that *we cannot really love other people if we do not learn to love ourselves first.* This idea has its own appeal and sounds like a legit thing to practice. But instead of believing it blindly, it might be a good idea to first look at some scientific studies related to this concept. The findings from a study conducted in 2017 state that compassion and self-compassion have quite different purposes and do not, in fact, go hand in hand with each other. They are targeted towards different goals in our lives and can be achieved using different mediums and practices. This might be a good time; then, to ditch the beliefs, we might be holding about any forced connections between compassion and self-compassion. However, having said that, it is actually of a lot of importance that we are kind to both ourselves and other people, as this does not just help to practice self-compassion but can also be a part of the larger project of changing our overall outlook towards life (as mentioned in one of the previous chapters). And what better way to start showing kindness and compassion than reassessing and changing the way you speak to the people in your life (this includes you too!)?

**How should we be speaking to the people around us?** When you are speaking to others, it is quite easy to show that you are overly compassionate, but what is actually important is the intention behind it. Here are a few ways in which you can be compassionate towards others while talking to them:

**Ask what they are looking for in the conversation:** Some people want a back and forth conversation, while some people prefer directly asking for advice, and even others might be looking for a conversation where they can just vent out without being interrupted or given any advice. One of the best ways to practice self-compassion with other people is to ask them what exactly they are looking for from their conversation with you at the very beginning. This is helpful in many ways. Such a prompt would help the other person in assessing their needs as much as it would help you tune your responses in a way that is appropriate for the situation. Also, it is important to communicate if you are not in the mind space for a certain kind of conversation (such as, maybe, giving advice to someone after you've had a very long, tiring day) so that nobody channels their energy is a way that yields nothing helpful. Similarly, it is also a great practice to convey clearly to the other person what *you* are looking for in a conversation that you are initiating and asking first if they are comfortable with discussing that. This ensures that both of you are being compassionate and respectful to not just yourselves but also to each other.

**Circle back to important points:** It is quite easy for someone to lose track of what they were saying or what they mentioned at the beginning of the conversation as something important that they want to discuss. Especially in informal conversations, one topic leads to the other, and very often, there is no way you can trace how you ended up talking about something so different from what you both started with. However, in case something important has to be discussed, and the other person has already told you that, even if they lose track midway, it is ideal that you help them circle back to what they talk about. This can be done using directed prompts or by gently reminding them of any matters of importance. This shows that you are mindful of the other person's preferences and are interested in their perspective on what they consider to be important as well.

**Follow up if it is needed:** One of the best and most direct ways to show someone that you are a compassionate person is to follow up with them after your conversation has ended. For example, in case you told them you would read up on a certain topic, or finish the book you are currently reading, and get back to them to talk more about it, make sure that you are *actually* making that effort (or at least letting them know if you cannot). Keeping track of long drawn conversations can get tedious, but not following up is a really harmful practice as it would both make the other person's needs feel unimportant and invalidated and let yourself get away from a situation without having any accountability at all. Therefore, if you have made a promise to someone to follow up with them, to catch up later, simply do that. Although it does not have to be the very next hour or next day, you need to make sure that it is not rolling into the next year either.

**How should we be speaking to (and about) ourselves?**

It is slightly easier to practice compassion while talking to other people, but when we talk to ourselves, we often forget to extend similar amounts of kindness. That also happens because how we talk to others and to ourselves are inherently very different types of exchange. In any case, listed below are six points that would help you figure out how to speak to yourself while practicing self-compassion:

**Be aware of how you are defining yourself:** What is your identifier? What really defines yourself? Pay close attention to how other people introduce themselves, and you will get a good idea about which of the many identities they have do they associate the most with. In the same way, be aware of how you are introducing yourself and which identity you are giving priority to- your occupation, where you come from, your educational institute, or something completely else. Once you are conscious about how you select your identifiers, then you are more likely to be careful and selective about the terms you are using to define yourself, instead of simply following a format other people are using. Being aware of how to define yourself makes sure that you pick out which are the attributes about yourself that you really want to put out there, which helps in self-assessment, which is always an act of great care and compassion.

**Replace affirmations with realistic questions:** Instead of mindlessly saying "I can do that!" to every single thing that comes your way, try taking a step back and asking yourself this question instead- "Can I do that?" more often. This will help you set better and more realistic goals and will also make sure that you are constantly aware of your capabilities and the mind space you have available. Asking yourself this question at the beginning of any project, any commitment, or any task is important as it will also give you a good sense of exactly how much effort do you need to put into the task at hand, as otherwise a blanket "yes, I can" statement might not be very helpful in understanding the nature and necessity of all the things you have to tend to.

**Try to use energizing language:** This one might sound pretty obvious but try to incorporate more energetic and positive language when you are speaking to yourself, and especially try to avoid any form of self-deprecation. Using energizing language will, in a way, make sure that the associations your mind is making while talking to your own self is mostly positive and full of hope. Although it is absolutely impossible to always practice this type of energy or positivity, allow yourself to practice as much as the situation permits (if it does at all) and be mindful about it even when you are not in a place to force yourself to be optimistic. While it is only natural to have a few bad days, it is very important to not lose sight of the larger picture- which here is to make positive associations about yourself, which would help you discard a lot of negative associations made about you in the past- either by you or by someone else- and replace them with neutral or optimistic ones instead. Having such an outlook is really helpful for practicing self-compassion.

**Set out clear instructions for yourself:** When you are trying to finish a task, you do not usually lay out a proper guideline in front of you as you would for other people if they were working on the same thing. Such an attitude towards ourselves comes from the idea that since we are informed about something, we are well equipped to navigate through the entire process. And what might end up happening if we do not set out instructions is that you might get overwhelmed, or there might be a problem in execution simply because you were so busy with the bigger picture, you did not pay enough attention to all the smaller parts which make it up. Therefore, while you are doing a task, make sure to talk yourself through it next time onwards. By talking through, I mean that you should give yourself step-by-step directions. Once you are clear about what needs to be done to proceed to just the very next step and not the overall goal, it would be much easier to work on it with more ease and fewer anxieties.

**Make sure your words are not being rephrased:** This is a step that is not completely about you but also involves other people. While you are talking to yourself or about yourself in front of others, it is also important to take note of how the things you are saying (mostly about yourself and your expectations) are being passed on. You should make sure that your words are not being rephrased so that you are held responsible for expectations you did not set yourself out to meet in the first place. Therefore, it is not just important to be kind while talking to yourself; it is also important to ensure that other people are also talking about you in a way that you permit. It is actually a good practice to politely correct other people or rephrases their words in case they have misinterpreted something you have said or are simply not careful enough to reproduce them with care.

**Practice saying "stop" to negative thoughts:** We all have negative thoughts from time to time. For all of us, negative thoughts are very intrusive. Negative thoughts, no matter how tiny and trivial they are, can have a very deep and lasting impact on our feelings as self-images. Therefore, a good practice while talking to yourself is to learn how to say "stop" to any invasive negative thought. There have been various studies that have demonstrated how saying "stop" upon facing an ugly thought have helped people better manage their anger and frustration and just deal with the situation better overall, with a reported improvement in the quality of sleep they get at night. Blocking out negative thoughts help us avoid the long, long process of revisiting things repeatedly in our head and try to conjure the worst-case scenario in case the thought in mind comes true. However, it is also important to block out all negative thoughts or anxieties altogether; the focus here instead is to stop ourselves from worrying excessively without a concrete reason.

**Are you enjoying this book? If so, I'd be really happy if you could leave a short feedback on Amazon, it means a lot to me! Thank you**

https://www.amazon.com/Self-Compassion-Workbook-accept-yourself-ebook/dp/B08XMFBXK7

# GET THE AUDIOBOOK VERSION
## of "Self Compassion Workbook"
## FOR FREE WITH A 30 DAY AUDIBLE TRIAL

Following this link for USA :

https://www.audible.com/pd/B0933NFF4M/?source_code=AUDFPWS0223189MWT-BK-ACX0-252040&ref=acx_bty_BK_ACX0_252040_rh_us

Following this link for UK:

https://www.audible.co.uk/pd/B0934M3D9G/?source_code=AUKFrDlWS02231890H6-BK-ACX0-252040&ref=acx_bty_BK_ACX0_252040_rh_uk

# Chapter 5:

## Self-Image –

**Recognizing that the only thing you can control is yourself and letting go of self-criticism**

It is really hard, almost impossible, to be compassionate towards your own self if you are constantly being weighed down by the burden that is self-criticism. Self-criticism comes almost naturally to us and is hard to get rid of completely. It has a really great impact on how we see and think of ourselves and how we value ourselves in terms of our talents and capabilities. While being absolutely not critical of yourself is not preferred (because being blind to your flaws is not the best idea either, although it does serve short term escapist purposes), a neverending stream of self-criticism is not very likely to be beneficial to anybody's self-esteem. Since self-compassion largely depends on the changes we are making in our lives in terms of how we regulate our thoughts and emotions, a good way to get better at it is to acknowledge that self-criticism has some harmful effects on everybody and should not be a coping mechanism we end up constantly resorting to. Since we only have control over our own actions, we might end up criticizing ourselves a lot of time for things that were not even our responsibility in the first place. If something was beyond our control, then there is little to no point in blaming ourselves for its consequences, as we have already discussed in some of the previous chapters in this book as well.

It is not easy to bring about a change overnight in the way we look at how we function. But if practiced gradually, this change is quite an easy one to fit into our lives. Since the payback is genuinely positive, it also becomes a habit over time and can turn into a changed mindset eventually. Listed below are a few tips on the changes you need to bring about in your mindset so that you can try and understand how to avoid mindless self-criticism:

**Avoid using self-criticism as a tool for motivation:** Directly or otherwise, a lot of us end up using self-criticism as a way to motivate ourselves to achieve certain goals. Being very critical of ourselves can, in fact, be a way of pushing ourselves through something we are doing and making sure we get to the end of it (because, yes, or else we would hurl more criticisms at ourselves, of course). Although this might work most of the time, it really is not the best idea to use self-criticism as a form of negative reinforcement since it is not a constructive way of motivating ourselves or judging our progress. Instead of using criticism as a way to motivate ourselves, it might be a better idea to direct some of the criticism (in case you cannot absolutely do away with that) as an afterthought once you are done with the task, as a sort of feedback instead of a continuous thought eating at you while you are trying to focus on a task. But even in this case, make sure you are actually using it towards your development and not just as a ploy to motivate yourself just enough to check the next thing off your task list.

**Check if your self-criticism is accurate or not:** A lot of times, what happens is that the way in which we see and make assumptions about ourselves is not the most objective one. We have our own biases, insecurities, and prejudgments which guide how we assess ourselves, which automatically has an effect on the self-criticisms we level against ourselves at the same time. If our self-criticism is off the mark- due to the inherent biases that we hold- then it is natural that they are not ideal markers which we should use to judge ourselves. It is a nice idea to pause for a moment and try to figure out how accurate the self-criticism we subject ourselves to actually is, and then make changes to how we judge ourselves accordingly. If how we criticize ourselves is not very accurate, then the chances are that we will go on to set really unrealistic expectations and goals for ourselves because we would not have a rational parameter to judge what we are capable of doing. Misjudging our limits is one of the main reasons we fail to prioritize our needs, and exaggerated self-criticism makes an easy way to developing very incorrect judgments about ourselves.

**Criticize yourself, but only through writing:** If you are particularly feeling critical of something you have done, a healthier way to channelize it is to write it down. Thoughts and conversations with ourselves inside our head can get ugly in no time, and it is also really easy for negative feelings to spiral into other unpleasant emotions in a really short amount of time. This is exactly why writing down- or typing out- is helpful. It lets you be more objective and rational about the situation and also tries to make sure that you are not going down the rabbit hole of negative thoughts since the focus is fixed when you are writing something down. Apart from this, writing down about your feelings have been scientifically proven to be a good outlet for unresolved emotions and angst, so, during the process, you might also be able to come up with a solution to the problem at hand instead of just directing criticisms to your actions without finding a way to change things. Another reason why writing down can be helpful is because of the time constraints. If you feel like taking your time out to jot down the criticisms you have is not really worth your time, then the chances are that fixating on the issue in the first place was actually not worth your time and mental space, as well.

**Learn what your triggers are:** Every individual has their set of triggers. In this case, triggers would include certain things that are sensitive towards and which will make you resort to self-criticism easily. This trigger can also be a person or an event you need to show up for; any sort of real or perceived exposure can be termed as a trigger. If you carefully go back to the times where you criticized yourself excessively and try to understand what had led to that bout of self-doubt and judgment, high chances are that you will be able to find a pattern behind it. Once you can see a pattern, finding out what your possible triggers are would not be very hard. After identifying your triggers, you also need to make sure that you are either avoiding exposure to these triggers, or are well equipped in advance to deal with the emotional vulnerability you might be facing if compelled to interact with a triggering situation.

**Try to see both sides of the story:** You are prone to criticizing yourself because you possibly see only one side of the story- the side which tells you what has gone wrong and what can be further improved. But no story has just a single side to it. Instead of spending your time and energy picking out flaws in yourself, what mind help in both understating the situation better as well as being more compassionate towards yourself is to try and see what the other sides to this story are. Are we other people respond to some extent for the outcome? Was the situation in your favor, or was there a leveled playing field? Was the outcome the best case possible scenario despite you giving your best to it? Analyzing all of these (and more) might result in you going a lot easier on yourself as if it gives you a more all-round picture of the scenario and makes you aware that not everything we are forced to deal with is directly under our own control.

**Try being more actively mindful:** If you are more present in the situation and more mindful about things, then the chances are that you would be less critical about yourself. This is because when you are mindful, you are more aware of the situation and are actively trying to ground yourself, keeping in mind everything else going on around you, which are also affecting the situation in one possible way or the other. This would naturally help us perceive the situation in a more nuanced way. The less clarity we have about something, the more are the chances of us having negative self-assessment in that situation because we do not exactly know what or who to put the blame on. Therefore, being more mindful about the things you are engaging in and the manner in which you are engaging will really help you out in understanding the role you have to play given the larger scheme of things.

**Look at the better things about you:** Yes, there might be many things about you which you would want to criticize, but for a change, it is a really helpful practice to do quite the opposite of self-criticism, and finding out what are the qualities about yourself which you absolutely cherish and are proud of. This will help you gain a better understanding of your strengths and weaknesses overall; it will help you realize that although there are things about yourself which can do with some improvement, there are also many positive attributes to you which you have consciously worked towards, and therefore deserve some praise. Having such an understanding will also help you come to terms with the fact that it is impossible for a person to excel in all fields, which is why shortcomings are only natural, and they do not deserve continuous criticism, especially from your own self.

**Practice showing gratitude to yourself:** This might not sound like a worthwhile exercise at first. After all, being thankful to yourself does not seem to make all that sense as it does to be grateful towards the people around you who impact your lives. However, you must remember that the person who has the biggest and the most long-lasting impact on your life is nobody else but you. You choose to wake up every day and actively be there for yourself as much as possible, for which you definitely deserve some acknowledgment, at the least.

One of the most important ways of being kind to your own self is to show gratitude to it on a regular basis. Expressing gratitude to yourself is different from finding out what are the good qualities in you. Gratitude is even more organic and can stem from the smallest of things, regardless of it being a specific advantage or flaw about your personality. Maintaining a gratitude journal can be a good and effective way to document how you are showing gratitude to yourself. Take 5 minutes out from your schedule every day to write down one thing you are grateful about- it can be anything, from your resilience to sit through an uninteresting lecture to the self-control you showed in saving up some extra money during a month, just pick one thing out, and it works the best if your choices are not revolving around bigger life decisions. Our trajectory in life is usually most affected by the smaller, seemingly unimportant things we do and choices we make, and if we start identifying and making a note of them, we would naturally be more appreciative of ourselves.

In this chapter, we have briefly gone over how self-criticism is linked to self-compassion. Next, we have discussed why it is important to cut down on (and try to get rid of) self-criticism, followed by a detailed list of suggestions for actually minimizing the amount of criticism you direct towards yourself. Although these steps are only a few, if you make an effort to incorporate them into your daily life, you are bound to notice an improvement in how you see yourself soon enough. Once you are cutting down on the unnecessary negative self-talk, you have a lot more allowance to practice self-compassion and kindness.

# Chapter 6:

# Daily practices –

# Stress response, how to eliminate negative energy and care for yourself

In a fast-paced world like this, we are constantly under great pressure to show up and deliver. Excessive pressure can often make us lose sight of our goals and introduce a lot of negative energy into our lives. This negative energy, along with the already looming stress, amounts to the point where we feel not just tense but also extremely overwhelmed with our life. This building up of negative energy can also push us towards burnout. In order to control our responses to stress, we need to include different self-care practices in our daily life. Practices like these will also help check the negative energy and help us keep track of our short and long-term objectives.

**How does our body react to stress?**

Although we usually attach a negative meaning to stress, it can actually be both positive and negative. Eustress- or positive stress- is a type of stress which acts to our benefit and is helpful for us. Therefore, we need to keep in mind that not all stress is bad and that some amount of stress is actually required for us to perform. However, the more common type of stress which we know about is called distress, or negative stress. When we are discussing stress in this chapter, we will be talking about this second kind of stress. All of us are affected by stress. Some of us do not notice the signs at once, and some of us quicker to spot them, but regardless, we are all driven by stress. Stress has lasting effects on our physical and mental health, and if stress is not regulated in a healthy way, our body starts reacting to stress at the smallest of triggers on an almost daily basis. Stress also means different things to different people, which is why a lot of symptoms of stress are not very universal- some people may notice some signs in greater degrees than others, and so on. How our bodies react to stress, therefore, is not easy to spot, as these symptoms come along with a lot of other very common physical conditions as well. Too much stress, especially unchecked, can and will make us fall sick. Physical and mental exhaustion is one of the most obvious signs of stress. Other physical signs can include headache, nausea, joint pain, extreme fatigue, loss of appetite, trouble sleeping, dry mouth, restlessness, and chest pain. When we are stressed, it targets our immune systems directly, which is why it also makes us vulnerable to other things such as cough and cold. When it comes to mental health, the effects of stress can be very long-drawn; some of the more immediate signs can be easy forgetfulness, procrastination, excessive and constant worrying, having trouble focusing, racing thoughts, increased pessimism, and lack of proper judgment skills. Increased dependence on substances such as alcohol, tobacco, and drugs are also signs of stress overload.

**How to reduce stress by taking care of yourself?**

Perhaps the main aim of self-care is to keep our stress under control. Since stress has a very extensive impact on us, stress-management is something which we must practice on our own. Investing our time and efforts into mindful self-care is a great way to get started on this. To manage stress, our self-care needs to include self-calming practices so that we can avoid being emotionally overwhelmed or extremely anxious. Self-calming practices work their way through our bodies to control how negative stress manifests itself. Through these practices, changes are introduced in our central nervous system (also known as the autonomic nervous system). This system controls important bodily functions such as heartbeat, breathing, and digestion. The central nervous system is further divided into the sympathetic and parasympathetic divisions. While the former is in charge of triggering stress responses, the latter division helps calm us down. This part of our nervous system is where self-calming is targeted. Some of the self-calming practices which can directly and noticeably have a positive effect on our parasympathetic nervous system include meditation, muscle relaxation, yoga, and intentional breathing. All of these help us manage stress quite effectively.

But apart from these specific practices designed to achieve mindfulness and the sense of calm, there are certain other prompts and practices we can try to make a part of our lives so that self-care is always on our list of priorities. Some of these are listed below.

**Physical self-care:** Stress has a direct effect on our body, so this section takes care of how we can practice self-care in order to prevent our bodies from coming under excessive stress. Tracking our sleeping and eating patterns carefully, identifying if there has been a change- and if yes, what can be the cause behind it- or not, actively investing in some physical activities (which can even just be cleaning our rooms), and noticing how our body reacts to certain situations in order to understand our triggers better are all ways of practicing physical self-care. These can have a very long-lasting positive impact in terms of how we can manage and combat stress.

**Mental self-care:** We all have our passions, and it is very important to make time for activities that mentally stimulate us, which make us feel connected to things and causes that we are passionate about so that we have something positive to come back to after a hard day. Mental self-care practices require us to make time for these activities so that we can keep our minds recharged from time to time. Our minds have only a limited capacity, and once it is saturated, it might be very difficult to continue with regular functioning without feeling absolutely overwhelmed and stressed. This is exactly why actually finding some time out from our schedule to do what we really like to do- be it reading a book, learning how to play guitar, or just catching up on a favorite show- is an essential and not a 'waste of time,' as many of us have been made to believe at some point of our lives.

**Social self-care:** People can be very draining, and interacting with people with a negative attitude and mindset can be really aggravating to our stress responses. Social self-care involves us being very mindful about whom we are choosing to spend time with and what is the nature of our engagement. It also requires us to become familiar with certain social activities which we enjoy doing and then actively making time to do the same with close friends and family (given that they are not draining). Self-care is not just limited to cutting negative people and energy from our lives, but it also includes trying to consciously find more ways to infuse positive energy as well.

**Emotional self-care:** Our emotions form a very big part of our everyday activities. It is natural to have certain pent-up emotions within ourselves from time to time, but emotional self-care practices remind us to check whether we have healthy outlets to properly express our emotions- positive or negative- or not. Having a proper outlet for our emotions is extremely important when we are dealing with excessive stress and its effects. A lot of times, even we are unaware of the exact emotion we are experiencing, and not having a channel to let it out can have very serious ill effects on our mental health. Seeking professional help is also a highly recommended way of taking care of ourselves and actually making it a priority to invest in our mental wellbeing.

**Spiritual self-care:** We can practice spiritual self-care even if we are not religious or identify as a 'spiritual' person. This aspect takes care of the larger picture at hand. What is our purpose in life? Are we actively engaging in experiences from which we are benefitting from? Asking ourselves these questions and identifying our feelings can be the first step in recognizing the many possible things we are stressing over but which hold no immediate or long-term importance for us. Once we recognize this, we can then take further steps on how to eliminate those from our lives, but even identifying them needs a lot of conscious energy and honestly on our part, which forms what spiritual self-care is addressed towards.

**Stress and negative energy**

Negative energy does not have a fixed definition. It is very subjective, but it is also very impactful. Negative energy can sit at the back of our minds and constantly bother us without us properly identifying it and dealing with it the way in which we should. Negative energy can come from different sources. Our immediate surroundings- places, people, and the environment- is one of the biggest contributing factors for negative energy. One of the immediate effects of negative energy is that it will leave you completely drained- both physically and psychologically. Dealing with fatigue is difficult, and it makes us even more tired in the process. The negative energy which is causing us fatigue is basically linked with how stress manifests itself in our bodies and lives. Another really significant source of negative energy which we often forget to notice is negative self-talk. Stress affects our judgment skills (as discussed above), which makes us develop a wrong perception of ourselves in our minds. This makes us pile up heaps of self-criticism and negative self-talk on our own selves, which is really hard to deal with. Negative self-talk affects us directly and also makes us more vulnerable to others criticizing us since our guards are completely down when it comes to receiving any sort of feedback or comments in this case. And when others criticize us and our barriers are already relaxed, instead of working on how to fix our mistakes,

we find it the easiest to blame ourselves even more. Since this is such a vicious cycle, negative energy- which is caused due to too much stress- ends up exposing us to even more stress in return. Some signs which point towards having a negative energy around us include:

**We are constantly found to be complaining:** When the negative self-talk manages to escape our head and tries to find some sort of release, it turns into complaints- long, vocal, neverending complaints from us. Through complaining or nagging, we are not dealing with negative energy in the right way. We are putting them out there in front of other people, which can both affect them as well as affect you through their responses to this action.

**We are critical of everything:** Negative energy also manifests itself through constant criticism and hypersensitivity. Harbouring negative energy within ourselves also tends to be reflected in ways in which the negativity is put out towards other people. This way, we often end up becoming unnecessarily critical of other things and people around us.

**We are always looking for distractions:** We tend to constantly look for distraction when there is too much negative energy surrounding us because we do not want to be left alone with our thoughts. If we are, then we are likely to fixate over what has been stressing us out, but due to mental clutter, these thoughts are not the most constructive ones. This is a very big reason why if we are bogged under plenty of negative energy, it becomes hard for us to focus on one thing, and we end up looking for constant distractions. Often, these distractions are also really mindless activities, so we do not gain anything from them in the long run and often end up regretting wasting a lot of our time and energy on them. However, the fault is not ours; this redirecting of our energy becomes almost necessary when we have too many things going on and causing stress in our mind, all of which demand a lot of attention.

**There has been a change in our eating and sleeping patterns:** As mentioned already, under the signs of stress, negative energy is also reflected in a sudden and drastic change in our eating and/or sleeping patterns. We tend to overeat or suddenly lose appetite; find it very hard to sleep or get out of bed- but are never satisfied with the sleep we are getting. Food and rest are supposed to be the fuels that our body needs to function. If they cannot serve their purposes, it just means that our body is being weighed down by a lot of other external factors, which is altering our normal schedules.

## How to eliminate negative energy?

The best and most effective way to cut negative energy off is by channelizing our energy more mindfully towards sources of positive energy in our everyday life. This includes small changes in our own thoughts, behavior, and actions which add up to bring a noticeable shift in our overall response to stress. It is important to keep in mind that negative energy affects both our mind and our body, which is why we need to pay special attention to our mental as well as our physical health when we are trying to eliminate negative energy and its impact on our routine.

Here are a few ways in which we can try to eliminate the negative energy from our daily lives:

**We need to cut down on complaints:** Criticism sure has its purpose, but it helps a lot to cut down on how much we tend to complain- mostly about things that are not even in our control- while we are stressed. Since we cannot fix much of the things we are complaining about, constantly having them at the back of our minds will not help us divert our undivided attention to anything else. This is also how the effect negative energy has on us can become very long drawn. Only complaining without any action makes no sense, but the action is often not in our hands. Therefore, in such situations, it is best to accept that there are certain things that we cannot control, and not having control over these is absolutely alright and not something we must worry about.

**We can take up meditation:** Meditation is the best way of practicing mindfulness. Although taking up something completely new might sound daunting to a lot of people, meditation is not just easy to learn but is also easy to keep up with. Meditation helps us focus on ourselves and lets us spend time with ourselves so that we get to know our minds and body better. It is a great antidote to the negative impacts of stress. Physically, meditation helps to relax our muscles, controlling our fight or flight response (which is triggered by a high-stress situation) and decreasing our stress hormones. If practiced regularly, meditation can really bring about a great change in our lives by actively inculcating positive energy to replace the negative energy created because of excessive stress.

Meditation can be easily practiced at our own convenience using different varieties of dedicated apps and software to guide beginners.

**We must keep our body active:** Another important way of enhancing positive energy is to keep our bodies moving on a daily basis. This can be done by going on a walk, practicing yoga, or even practicing a favorite activity- such as dancing or cycling for half an hour every day. Lethargy breeds even more negative energy, so we need to keep our bodies up and running- even if for a little while- to break the hold stress has on us. There are a lot of physical benefits of having an active lifestyle as well. It helps to flush out toxins from our body, activates our subtle energetic system, and takes your mind away from fixating on negative emotions by directing its attention to the continued need for greater amounts of oxygen during physical activities. Physical activities such as exercise are also scientifically proven to produce serotonin, which is our 'happy hormone' and tackles our negative energy and emotions in a healthy way.

**We should express gratitude:** As we have discussed in our previous chapters as well, gratitude becomes an essential thing to practice in order to incorporate more positive energy into our lives. Regularly showing how thankful we are to the different small things in our lives helps us remain grounded and shift our focus away from negative and intrusive thoughts. A lot of the negative energy weighing us down is rooted in our belief that everything is falling apart in our lives, and there is no way out in sight. But expressing gratitude reminds us about the many positive things in our lives, which we often take for granted, and slowly, our minds are attuned in a way that we naturally start to try and see the positive aspect of things, and not obsess over the impact of negative energy.

**We must redirect our self-talk:** It really helps us to cut down on negative self-talk and take a more kind and understanding approach towards ourselves, much like we would do for a friend of ours. If we can allow ourselves to escape the burdens of getting everything right all the time through positive self-talk, we will be able to easily eliminate a lot of- if not all the negative energy, which makes us less resourceful and optimistic. Negative self-talk often also sets up very unrealistic expectations for ourselves, mostly out of anxiety or guilt. But we must cut ourselves some slack and be very realistic while setting goals and telling ourselves how much we can achieve and how well we can do that.

In this chapter, we first discussed the different signs of stress and the ways in which our bodies react to excessive stress. Then, we spoke about the relationship between stress response and self-care. After this, we also discussed how stress leads to the breeding of negative energy in our lives, finally glancing over a few ways in which this negative energy can be kept under check.

# Chapter 7:

# Daily practices –

# Meditation techniques and breathing exercises, to start and end the day for better sleep

Research has proven that almost 30 to 50% of all adults have problems sleeping. This problem is often related to the levels of stress they are experiencing in life, which is why effectively controlling stress can have a great positive impact on how to get better sleep, which is absolutely integral for functioning properly on a day-to-day basis. Stress is related to sleep because a higher level of stress can very easily cause us to get highly anxious and restless, increasing our tension levels and naturally making it harder for us to get a good night's worth of sleep. For some people who already have insomnia or other issues related to sleeping, stress can only make it much worse. Different relaxation techniques have the potential to help us have a better and more peaceful sleep. Meditation is one of the go-to techniques for combating stress and getting better sleep. It is a very effective way to relax because it is also very beginner-friendly. You do not need to spend a lot of time, money, or effort to get started with, or even master, the art of meditation. It is a very easy practice if you are simply mindful, which is all it takes to start your journey towards getting better at resting.

## How can meditation help us get better sleep?

Meditation helps us be more mindful of our circumstances and help us reduce our stress, which naturally has an effect on how easily we are able to rest our mind and body and sleep. When we meditate, we also set ourselves towards having better control over our autonomous nervous system, which makes it easier for us to relax at our own will. This part of our body also controls how easily we can be awakened from sleep, and having better control over it can help us regulate our sleep cycles in an efficient way. There are different other scientific ways in which meditation can help us with our sleep problems, some of which include:

- It decreases our blood pressure, thus making it easier to relax
- It increases different hormones- such as serotonin and melatonin- which are needed for relaxation and thus can help us worry less and sleep better
- It controls and regulates our heart rate and helps reduce it
- It also activates several parts of our brain which control how we sleep

Other than these, meditation also promotes better sleep by initiating several changes in our body while we meditate, which are similar to what we experience during the early cycles of our sleep, and therefore, it becomes easier for us to transition into a state of more mindful relaxation. No matter if we are beginners at meditation or not, and regardless of which meditation technique we pick for ourselves, there are a few pointers which we must be aware of before starting with meditation. Some of these pointers are as follow:

**Find a quiet area:** Meditation is a quiet activity. It usually is something you do on your own while you are on your own (unless there are other people around who want to do the same thing), which is exactly why you must find a really quiet area to meditate on your own. This area can be your own bedroom or a secluded study corner. In case you are meditating for better sleep, meditating on your bed is a very good option as well, as long as you are not sharing your bedroom with roommates or the like. Meditation, no matter how hard you try, might yield absolutely no results if the area around you is cluttered, noisy, and full of distractions. So, it is the best thing to pick a quiet spot for you to get into the zone, and it would also eventually help you to rest and sleep better, naturally.

**Turn your phone off:** This one is an absolute no-brainer. Your phone is not just a huge source of distraction; it is also a source of blue light which harms our biological sleeping cycle. Turning the phone off helps us to focus single-mindedly on one thing at hand, and it is also very hopeful to steer clear of the endless incoming mails and overflowed inboxes once in a while. With a non-stop inflow of notifications, we might always feel like there is something on our mind, that we have left something unattended which requires our urgent attention, and that is one of the biggest reasons we keep checking our phones every five minutes, eventually falling down the digital rabbit hole and finding it absolutely impossible to get our mind off stuff and *really* relax.

**Set up the atmosphere:** Once your phone is off, you might also want to go ahead and turn the lights off (keeping a dim light on might be a good idea, though), cleaning your room, bed, and table, and getting rid of any visual clutter which might be an obstacle for you to relax. Some people also want to take a shower right before they meditate or go to bed as it is helpful to calm them down physically. Try experimenting with a few different things, such as scented candles, fragrance diffusers, ASMR, and calming sounds (many relaxing playlists are available online- on different streaming platforms and even on YouTube). Try and see what works the best for you and what really helps to intensify the full effect of meditation for you, helping you to get better and more peaceful sleep overall.

**Remember the reason:** You are not meditating for the sake of it or just because you wanted to try out a fun new activity. Remember the actual reason you started to meditate (or wanted to do so) in the first place so that you can keep yourself motivated and are clear about the outcome you are expecting out of your meditation session.

**Do not overwhelm yourself:** There might be one too many meditation tutorials out there for you to get overwhelmed about, which is why this last tip is really important to keep in your mind. Like every other activity (especially the ones marketed as 'self-care'), there might be a lot of unnecessary pressure to ace it right away and to get the most out of the tutorials and the instructions you might be consulting. However, meditation works differently for everyone, and therefore, the end results are also different for everyone. Instead of getting carried away by the appeal of it and trying to perfect it at the first go, it will actually benefit you a lot more if you are mindful about how you are trying to be more mindful, i.e., meditation. Getting overwhelmed will just add on even more to the dress you are already under, which will actually backfire when it comes to helping you to get better sleep and start a better day.

**Some meditation and breathing techniques for better sleep**

The lives we lead are very fast-paced and demanding, and we are trained to live off deadlines, which makes it really difficult for us to unwind and relax at the end of the day. This is also why insomnia is on the rise, besides problems such as anxiety and stress- all of which collectively make sleeping a much difficult exercise. However, if you are struggling with getting proper sleep, it might help to remember that you are not alone in this. According to a study conducted by the American Sleep Association (or

ASA), nearly half of all Americans face either short-term or chronic sleeping problems.

Nasal breathing exercises are great for de-stressing, both short and long-term. A study conducted in 2013 has demonstrated that people who have regularly tried some form of a nasal breathing exercise have reportedly felt less stressed afterward. Following the same path, if you are looking for some breathing techniques which will help you out with better sleep, look no further! This list of breathing techniques and exercises might be the one that you have been looking for all this while:

**The three-part exercise:** This breathing exercise is one of the easiest ones on this list. For this, start with a long and deep inhale. Next, exhale completely. While you are exhaling, focus on how your body is feeling throughout this process. The focus should be on the feeling and not on the act of breathing. Repeat this a few times. While you are repeating, adjust your breathing in a way so that your exhales are twice as long as your inhales. These are the simple three parts of this exercise, and in spite of being simple and easily doable, the results of this breathing exercise are excellent!

**Box breathing technique:** In this technique, the focus is placed on the oxygen that your breath is pulling in and pushing out through repeated cycles. For this technique, you will first have to sit down with your back straight, then breathe in gently, followed by an attempt to push all the air that is filling your lungs at one go as you exhale. While you count up to 4 in your mind, use your nose to inhale slowly. Next, fill your lungs up with more air by each passing number that you count. Now, hold your breath while you again count to 4 in your head. Use your mouth to exhale slowly, and keep your focus on getting all the oxygen- that is in your lungs- out. This technique is a very common practice during meditation as it is really popular to find mental peace and focus.

**The 4-7-8 exercise:** For this technique, you will first have to open your lips slightly and let them part a little. Exhale completely, and make a strong whoosh sound while you exhale. Next, press your lips together for around four seconds while you steadily inhale only through your nose. Now hold your breath for exactly seven seconds. Next, exhale, but this time- for eight seconds (hence, the 4-7-8 name for this technique), and do not forget to make the whooshing time while you exhale. Repeat this exercise four times as you get started; practice until you can easily get through eight repetitions.

**Pranayama breathing technique:** This one is a well-known breathing exercise. For this, first, close your eyes. With your eyes closed, breathe in and out in a steady rhythm, deeply. Cover both of your ears using your hands. Next, position your index fingers in a way that they are placed one on top of each of your eyebrows, and the rest of the finger is over your eyes. Apply a little pressure on both sides of your nose using your fingers while keeping the focus on the area around your brows. While you do this, keep your mouth closed. Breathe out only using your nose, and try to make the 'om' sound while you exhale. Repeat the entire process at least five times for a change in your state of mind.

**Kapalbhati breathing technique:** For this technique, you will have to sit in a position which you are comfortable in while keeping your spine straight. Keep your hands on your knees, and make sure your palms are facing the sky upwards. Now, take in a deep breath. Next, exhale, and contract your stomach while you are breathing out. Force yourself to breathe out in short bursts. You can also keep a hand on your belly to feel how your abdominal muscles are contracting during your exhale. While you are releasing your abdomen, air should automatically flow into your lungs. Finish one round of Kapal Bhati by repeating this exercise 20 times. Once one entire round has been completed, gently close your eyes and try to sense how your body is feeling. Complete the exercise by finishing two more rounds completely. More details about this exercise have been outlined on the Art of Living website.

**Alternate nasal breathing technique:** This technique is also a part of the pranayama breathing techniques and is sometimes known as the *nadi shodhana pranayama* exercise. To begin with, sit down with your legs crossed. Keep your right hand on your knee while the thumb of your left hand is placed against your nose. First, exhale completely; after that, close your right nostril. Now, exhale through your left nostril. Repeat the procedure- open your right nostril, close the left one, and exhale through the right one. Carry on the process five times, and make sure that the last time you exhale, it is done through your left nostril.

**The Papworth exercise:** In the Papworth technique, you will train your diaphragm in a way that it can breathe in and out more naturally. To start, assume a straight posture- this can be done either by sitting up straight or even by lying down if you are trying to do this to get better sleep. Methodically take deep breaths in and out. Count up to 4 each time that you breathe in – be it through your mouth or your nose – as well as when you exhale, which must be done only using your nose. While you breathe, keep your focus on how your abdomen is rising and falling, and notice how you can listen to the sounds of your breathing coming deep down from your stomach. This is a method of relaxation proven to be especially helpful for people who face problems with sighing and/or yawning very frequently.

**Buteyko breathing exercise:** This is another breathing technique that is very helpful for people facing problems with getting proper sleep. In this exercise, you need to sit on your bed with your mouth closed gently while you must breathe through your nose for about 30 seconds at a natural pace- neither too hurried nor too slow. Next, make your breathing more intentional as you breathe in and out of your nose. Now use your thumb and forefinger to pinch your nose shut- during this time, keep your mouth closed as well- until you feel the absolute urge to take another breath. Use your nose to take a deep breath in, and then exhale while your mouth remains closed all this time. This exercise is a good one to bring hyperventilation under control and regulate or maintain a normal, healthy pattern of breathing.

**Diaphragmatic breathing technique:** For this technique, first lie down on your back. Keep your knees either bent over a pillow or use a chair for sitting on. Position one hand on your stomach, flat, and the other one on your chest. Use your nose to take in short and deep breaths while you feel your abdomen rise and fall using your hand placed over. Keep your lips pursed and breathe out through them in the next step. As you feel your chest and abdomen, you will be eventually able to breathe in a way that your chest is no longer rising and falling frantically, and you can hold a steady motion. This breathing technique helps in strengthening your diaphragm; it also lowers your oxygen needs.

**Breathing while repeating a mantra:** This is a good practice to turn to if and once you are well-versed with the art of abdominal breathing. To do this effectively, either lie down or sit up in a position that is comfortable for you. Take a deep breath through your abdomen, and while inhaling, repeat a mantra to yourself. You can choose what works for you, but it can be useful to pick someone like "*inhale relaxation*" as you are starting off. Next, repeat a mantra along the lines of "*exhale tension*" while you breathe out through your abdomen. Take intentional pauses every time before you inhale or exhale. Continue this exercise for any amount of time between 5 and 10 minutes or until you start to feel adequately rested or sleepy. While you try these exercises out, it is important to keep in mind that different things work for different people, and you might have to go through a few misses to figure out which of these are the best fit for you and can guarantee you the result that you are expecting from your breathing exercises. Before beginning with any of the exercises, it is a good practice to try and ease yourself as much as possible, keep your eyes closed, block out as many distractions as you possibly can, and get into the proper mindset to shut your surroundings off and go to sleep. Your breath has healing powers, and once you are aware of that and are consciously focusing on it, it can be easy to divert straying thoughts in your mind to focus solely on the breathing patterns and on how they lead to good sleep. At the end of that day, regardless of which exercise works out the best for you and which one works out for you, you must focus on how breathing in certain ways can help you unwind, relax, and rest. Eventually, your goal should be to breathe in a more mindful, natural, and effective way so that you can seamlessly ease into a relaxed state of mind as and when you need to.

However, having said all of this, it helps to trackback to how relaxation is a very subjective process, and if meditation is not working for you, then the problem is not in you; you just have different de-stressing outlets which you would eventually figure out, and there is no reason to put any sort of pressure on yourself to try out breathing exercises if they are not proving to help you out with resting and sleeping better. To sum up, this chapter starts with discussing the relationship between meditation and sleep problems; it then talks about the scientific benefits of meditation and outlines a few tips to get started with meditation. Finally, it goes over a list of carefully curated meditation and breathing exercises that have been scientifically proven to help with problems related to relaxation and sleep.

# Chapter 8:

# Daily practices –

# Virtues and utilizing your surroundings

Our surroundings have a great impact on how we conduct ourselves and how well we are able to stick to our schedules. A cluttered surrounding usually points to a cluttered mind, and vice versa. A lot of times, we tend to treat our built environment as just something we need to adjust to but do not try to actively change it according to our conveniences, which is a mistake on our part. Since our surroundings have a direct effect on our lives and feelings, we should try and utilize our surroundings in a way that we can benefit the most out of it, and we can use it in a manner that ensures that we have control over what sort of impact we are allowing the surroundings to have on our daily lives.

## How do our surroundings affect us?

The ways in which we choose to surround ourselves can almost dramatically either lift our mood up or sink it. A lot of times, we are not aware of these impacts as we are not actively thinking about the surroundings that we are in. However, we need to be more mindful about our surroundings so that we can identify our triggers as well as what makes us feel content and calm- so that we can actively choose such surroundings and be a little kinder to ourselves (by choosing to avoid unwelcoming, unhappy, or anxious surroundings). These are just four out of many ways in which we are affected by our surroundings:

**Motivation:** Our motivations are heavily dependent on our surroundings. First of all, as we have already discussed in another chapter in this book, the people we choose to surround ourselves with majorly influence how we motivate ourselves and where we seek motivation from. Positive people help lift our moods up, while the negative company makes us feel dull and gloomy. However, even if we only look at our physical surroundings, we can see that there is a direct relationship between our motivation levels and them. For example, if the space around us is neat, organized, and tidy, we would be more driven to replicate the same amount of neatness and organization in the work that we do. In other words, a cleaner surrounding motivates us to be cleaner and more organized with the work which we are producing from being in that space. Other than this, we are also quick to associate certain colors with certain feelings. For instance, if blue is a color which I have on my bedroom walls, we might associate it to feeling drowsy and lethargic (i.e., the feeling of getting into bed), and then, wherever else we see the color blue, we catch ourselves slipping into that mood unchecked. If we can check and identify these minute triggers that we have, we can manage the effect our surroundings have on our motivations in a better and more informed way.

**Mood:** It goes almost without saying that our surroundings have a huge impact on our moods and emotions. Different elements in our physical surroundings, such as decor, color, light, and even temperature, can influence how we are feeling in that space. The decor of a room can highly influence how you feel when you are in that area. Some decor naturally makes you feel more welcome into space, while other forms of decor guard the space off, making you feel unwelcome and unwanted. It is hard to lift yourself up if you are not surrounded by welcoming features, which is why you might want to opt for a more open style of decor, one that you find welcoming. Some colors and some temperatures are connected to a more gloomy mood (such as shades of blue and colder temperatures); which is why if you are designing a workspace or a study area, you might want to avoid turning the heat down around that place or selecting colors which do not elevate your mood. Sometimes, brighter colors can also be too stressful for your eyes, making muted tones a better emotional regulator in your surroundings. We tend to have our 'happy' and 'unhappy' places but are not quick to register what are the factors about those spaces which elicit a certain emotion in us. These factors are often small, unnoticed details about the surroundings which together contribute to us feeling a certain way, and if we carefully dissect our happy/unhappy place keeping in mind these patterns, we will be able to get a good understanding of which aspects of our surroundings affect our mood, and how.

**Stress level:** This might not have been an easy connection to draw, but yes, our stress levels are also affected by the surroundings that we are in. Cluttered spaces are more likely to make us feel uneasy and anxious, resulting in a higher level of stress- especially if the cluttered area is not something we are familiar with (which means, we are most likely to still know what is kept where in our room even if it is untidy, but in someone else's room, it becomes harder for us to ground ourselves if the place is messy and disorganized, as we do not feel it to be an open place for our thoughts to flow smoothly as well). There have also been various studies in the field of color psychology which has linked certain colors and shades to different levels of stress and other related feelings.

**Social interactions:** A built environment is also where we interact with our peers, create certain bonds, and allow ourselves to freely express our thoughts and emotions. There are certain factors about a physical surrounding that make it easier than other spaces to be open for interaction. One of these factors is the seating arrangement of that area. If you are having an area designed which is ideally going to facilitate a lot of gatherings and interactions among people, then you must pay extra attention to the seating details in that space. Space should not just be welcoming, but it should also give the impression that it is designed to bring people together so that they can discuss things (this can be achieved, for example, by a semi-circle or circular seating arrangement instead of scattered chairs and seating areas across the place). The place should also be set up in a way that everyone present can get a good view of all the other members who are present with them in the area at that point of time so that nobody feels alienated or cut off during interactions.

## Utilizing our surroundings for maximizing productivity

If you are working from home and are finding it really difficult to adjust due to the current circumstances, then you might need to take a hard look around you and see what kind of environment you are working from. Our home is the place we associate with rest and relaxation and not work and productivity. This is why we have customized the surroundings of our house to help us feel at ease, which needs to be tweaked slightly so that the same space can also help us work better and stay more focused and organized. If this transition is turning out to be hard to navigate for you, then you have come to the right place. Listed below are a few ways in which you can better utilize your surroundings to suit it according to your work needs and to increase your productivity:

**Establishing a 'work only' area:** To separate your work area from the rest of your space is a real challenge, especially keeping in mind the current work from home scenario. It is very crucial to create a corner for you- however small it might be- which is dedicated solely to your work and nothing else. Work is the one and only association you should be making with that space so that it becomes easy for you to slip into the work mode whenever you settle into that space. If you have a dedicated study room, then setting up this corner should not be very difficult. However, in case you do not have the luxury of a study, take some time and put some effort into setting up a strictly work-only zone in your bedroom or living room. For this purpose, preferably choose a corner that is cut off from the rest of the room and is somewhat removed from most distractions so that it gives you the optimum chances of sitting down and focusing on nothing but your work.

**Have a running checklist:** Once you have set up your workspace, put up a running checklist in plain view so that you do not ever lose sight of the most important things that you need to get done during any given day. Often, what happens is that we pick up an important piece of information over an email or a work call but tend to forget it soon enough because there was nothing around us to write it down on. Even for these cases, a checklist can come in handy to make a quick note of running details. Although there are many apps that can help make your to-do lists, having the tasks written down on a piece of paper and in plain view can do miracles to the flow of your work. Make good use of a calendar, journal, or plain old post-it notes to keep your tasks listed out in your workspace.

**Cutting down background noise:** This one is a very important thing you must keep in mind while utilizing your surroundings. Background noise- often unnecessary and intrusive- is one of the main reasons for creating disturbance and interruptions while someone is trying to set their mind on something and work hard. If you are selecting a workspace for yourself, make sure that it has absolutely minimal exposure to background noise. This noise could range anything from the chirping of birds outside your window to the dull chatter of the television in the next room. It is a wise idea to distance yourself as much as possible from external sources of noise while you are trying to concentrate on your work. Although some people do love some natural sounds in the background as it helps them focus better, it might be a good idea for them to play the music on a device rather than counting on background noise, since that way, a pattern can be formed so that the workflow is directly associated with the nature playlist on their phones. And, if all efforts fail to reduce noise from outside, investing in a good noise-cancellation headphone might be an absolute lifesaver.

Background noise can also be a huge bummer if a lot of work is revolving around conference calls or Zoom sessions. In these cases, make sure to build a barrier between yourself and the rest of your house so that your workspace is cut off from the people around you. You might also want to consider putting up a 'do not disturb' sign near your workspace during hours that involve you being on the phone when you cannot really afford disturbances from the outside.

**Decluttering the space, you work in:** Both physical and digital declutter are essential things to maintain in your workspace. Sitting down to work in a space that visibly looks clear and non-congested is a huge game-changer; plus, it also saves you a lot of time and effort if you have to grab something while you are in a hurry. If you have a smaller workspace, then decluttering can bring about a significant change in the amount of physical space that would be available for you to work with. Decluttering does not just mean clearing out the unnecessary items and the junk; it also means having your stuff organized in a compact and efficient way so that you are making the most that can be done with the space and the furniture/wall spacing that you have. One of the best ways to utilize your surroundings for organizing effectively is by using smaller drawers and compartments instead of having everything piled on a larger clean surface (such as a tabletop). It also helps to have your drawers and shelves labeled so that you do not have to waste your time thinking about where you kept the exact file you need to pick out when you do not have a lot of time to go through all the shelves. You can even choose to go paperless (as much as possible) while you are decluttering so that while taking care of your personal surroundings, you are also making sure that your workspace is environment-friendly. Cutting down on unnecessary physical clutter (such as printouts, memos, and photocopies you do not need any longer) naturally brings about a positive change in the openness of the workspace that is available to us. It also gives you the sense that all your important documents are in one place- saved and backed up – and do not run the risk of being misplaced or, worse, lost. It is also a good idea to send as much paper and plastic goods away for recycling as possible, which is why you can add a recycling bin to your workspace, which would help you to quickly sort through what has to be completely discarded versus what can be stored for future use in a different way.

**Maintain proper hygiene:** This one is a no-brainer, and even more so during the current conditions- do not forget to maintain proper hygiene in your workspace. Sanitize your devices and clean any exposed surfaces on a regular basis. It might be a good idea to actually sanitize laptop touchpads and keyboards on a daily basis, even since these are surfaces you touch multiple times in a day, every day. Keeping some wet wipes and tissues handy is also a good idea since they can come in especially handy in case you end up spilling something on your table or devices and can neatly clean up before any long-term damage is done. If you are especially working in a space which you share with other people, hygiene should be your utmost priority. Take care of your devices, but even more of any shared surfaces, and make sure to wash hands before and after you sit down to work as well, so that you are quick to get rid of any germs or impurities which you might have come in contact with during your work hours. Other than this, if you tend to have your lunch or snacks while you are at your desk (make sure you are only packing food which is easy to eat and clean up after, so that you do not waste any more time on that than you absolutely have to), make sure to be extra cautious with that as well, and clean up after your meal is over, ensuring that no leftovers or food waste are lying unattended.

**Get a dash of nature:** Since a lot of our work environments involve us working online and with devices for very long stretches every day, adding a dash of nature to your workspace can be a nice and welcome change. You can do this by adding a small potted plant on your desk or even by tapping into the rich world of fragrances by picking out a diffuser or a scented candle that has a natural, soothing smell. This sort of a foray into nature helps us break the monotony of our work environment, besides which natural smells can also help calm us down, which is an added benefit, given the hectic schedules we tend to run by. You can also try and add a dash of nature to your workspace by adding a rock collection or memorabilia that reminds you of the outdoors. Plus, it is a good chance for your eyes as well.

**Try and use natural light:** This one is not a must, but it is always better if you can use sources of natural light to work instead of artificial lamps and other lights. Natural lights do not have the harmful blue tint that comes from other sources of light, which means that they are gentler on our eyes and less prone to causing us a headache during long hours. Plus, natural lights also, of course, tend to save us a lot of money as well as are very eco-friendly. Picking a corner with natural light but minimal outside noise might be tricky, but in case natural light is an option for you, it is highly recommended that you go for it and make the most out of the daylight hours that you can.

Even when you are not using natural lights, be very careful about the shade and the intensity of the light you are picking out for your workspace, as they have a strong impact on your physical health as well as your flow of work. Warm tones of lights are safer for your eyes (especially if you tend to work for longer hours and in low light conditions), while bluish tinges of lights can cause problems regarding your sleep cycle and can even cause headaches in the longer run.

**Take regular breaks:** Breaks are a must when it comes to long work hours. But when you are taking a break, make sure that you actually physically get up and walk away from your work zone to a more relaxed part of the house or the workspace that you are using. If you are working out of your home, then having a place dedicated to spend time during these short breaks would be a great idea! It could be a comfortable couch or a reading chair or practically anything (apart from the bed, by all means) as far as you distancing yourself from your work zone. Another good way of using your surroundings is to create a clear work/rest distinction between the space you have been allocated so that there is no overlapping of boundaries. It is also a good idea to actually go outside of your house to take a break. Now, this does not mean that you are required to run errands or pick up groceries in between your works shifts, but just going out in the sun for a while to stretch your body out and experiencing a change in the light, sound, and other surroundings can be a quick little breather during long workdays. If you have a balcony or a patio, make sure to make good use of it by making them your quick, 10-minute break spots where you are not allowed to bring in work.

**Find a comfortable position:** Make sure you have found a position that gives ample rest to your back, neck, and shoulders. You can either use a normal desk or a standing desk, depending on how you prefer to work but ensure that the height and lumber you are using are well adjusted to suit your needs. An uncomfortable posture does not just result in less productivity but can also lead to long-term pains and distress in your body. Pick a corner of your house where you can feel absolutely comfortable with yourself, sitting at a stretch for multiple hours, and ideally, pick that corner to be your workspace if possible.

Ergonomics is key to finding a comfortable sitting position. Invest well in an ergonomic chair that is adjustable to different heights and angles so that you can not just find a suitable position but also have some options to choose from if you are switching between different tasks which require different degrees of intensity.

Also, make sure that your seating area has throws, pillows, or cushions so that you are well covered from back pains that might arise from sitting in a sedentary position for long stretches of time each day.

**Check your screen fatigue:** Another good way to utilize your surroundings well is to have enough buffer area for your eyes while you are working so that you can save yourselves from extreme screen fatigue. Since a huge chunk of our days is spent staring at a screen, it is important that we give our eyes some break as well. During this break, it helps a lot if we have a soothing, muted background to look at, which does not cause our eyes a lot of strain, and helps them to retain their focus as well. If you are designating a workspace for yourself, try and make sure that it mostly has muted, neutral tones and not very loud and vibrant colors, as they are not the most gentle on our eyes. To keep a check on the amount of your screen time, you can also use reminders on your device, which would make sure you are reminded from time to time to give your eyes a break from the laptop screen. Setting up a soothing screensaver can also impact the mood of your workspace drastically as it will help take your mind off all the work-related pressure for the tiny bits of time you set aside for yourself to relax and recharge. Monochrome images which do not have a lot of details are ideal for screensavers as they are both easy on your eyes and on the battery of your device as well.

**Keep yourself properly hydrated:** When you are sitting down to work at your desk, make sure you have enough supply to keep you hydrated for at least two to three hours. Have a water bottle or be close to a supply of water. Make sure that you are well connected to a water outlet or your kitchen so that refilling your bottle does not become a hassle for you. Staying hydrated is essential to remain energetic, so make sure you are planning out your workspace in a way that it has adequate access to connect you and your sources of hydration. Besides getting a water bottle, it is also not a bad idea to store up on some quick snacks to munch on in between work or study sessions. Make sure that you are choosing snack items that are not very flaky or messy and would not create a spillage. Certain items like nuts, dry fruits, and granola bars make very good hassle-free snacks and are also very easy to store, so it might be wise to stack a stash of these handy stacks in a drawer of your designated workspace.

**Build up a regular work routine:** Make sure that you use your surroundings to build yourself a step-by-step work routine so that it is not very difficult for you to transition into the work more every day. Your work routine can include basic steps like switching on the light dedicated to the work area or cleaning your desk; anything tangible that you do to the work environment will help you associate that place with your work so that it becomes easier for you to separate work from home while working within these restraints. A routine is important because it helps you build a habit that you can sustain in the long run, even if your immediate surroundings have been changed. Building a routine is also important because it makes use of all the aspects in your built surroundings and makes you aware of how you connect and interact with them, informing you in the process how and why they impact your mood and productivity. This chapter starts with focusing on the relationship our lives have with built surroundings and then moves on to discuss what are the different ways in which our surroundings can impact us. Next, it lists out twelve ways in which you could utilize the surrounding and set-up of your home for your work in a way which maximizes your productivity and helps your day-to-day lives.

# Chapter 9:

# Road mapping –

# Finding motivation in yourself

We have certain larger goals in life- buying a house, going on a world trip, investing in our dream car, and so on. However, all our big goals and victories are essentially made up of many smaller ones. We do not buy a house overnight; we plan, earn, and save systematically for a long period of time to be able to afford it someday. Therefore, we need to keep sight of smaller victories in life as they are the road to the bigger ones. If we do not allow ourselves the smaller victories, then we would not have enough motivation left in ourselves, which can drive us towards the bigger ones. To build a mindset which views smaller victories as an essential stepping stone on the path of fulfilling larger goals is a great way road mapping and building habits. Keeping ourselves motivated is, therefore, key to achieving what we aim for- in both the short and long term. We often turn to other external sources for motivation and forget in the process to find motivation from and within our own selves. This is not the best way of looking at things because external sources are temporary, and they only serve as effective sources of encouragement and validation for a limited amount of time. On the other hand, if we train ourselves to be the ones cheering us on and motivating us, it can be better ensured that we have motivation when we are feeling the most lost and down, and we can also be contained without turning to anyone else and their availability to fuel our own projects. Plus, learning to find motivation in ourselves is extremely important as it makes use of a lot of important qualities such as practicing gratitude, time-management, setting realistic priorities, and having clear intents- all of which add up to build a better version of us. There are many ways in which you can motivate yourself, but it might be a little tricky to figure out which of these ways are the most reasonable and tangible. It is alright to be a little confused about that, and if you are, then look no more! In case you are trying to find motivation in yourself when you are feeling lost and stuck, here are 20 practical ways in which you could help yourself out:

**Check your mindset:** If you feel stuck or demotivated, the reason might be a faulty mindset. It is important to reconsider, from time to time, how you really view goals, success, and failure. A clear, goal-oriented mindset is important to seek motivation for small and big victories.

Your mindset should focus on the process and not just the goal and should also be realistic in terms of what you want to achieve and how much you can possibly stretch yourself in order to achieve the same. It is difficult to undo or change your entire mindset overnight, but changing a little bit at a go is a practical thing that you can aspire towards.

**Dare to start small:** Everyone and everything needs to start small. That is why it is important that you dare to start small, with the very basics if you are feeling stuck and devoid of motivation. It might be possible that you have put too much pressure on yourself in terms of the larger picture, which you are very prone to visualizing. However, every big picture needs to be first broken down into smaller ones to make the project something that is realistically achievable. If you start small, you will have a better idea about how to go about finishing your tasks than to get carried away by bigger but more unrealistic end goals, which you might find hard to motivate yourself about.

**Visually organize your goals:** It really does help to motivate yourself if your goals are visually organized. If you can *see* what needs to be done, chances are higher that you will actually get them done. Breaking down your goals using visual aids such as mind maps or to-do lists is a good idea for tackling them one at a time and also for finding step-by-step motivation for yourself. Post-it notes are your best friends for organization and goal setting, and you can make use of them in multiple different ways- to write yourself affirmations, to break down task lists, or to prioritize what you are aiming for.

**Set goals that are smart:** Use the SMART way of goal setting if you are finding it a little hard to fetch motivation for the task at hand. This method of goal setting focuses on goals that are **S**pecific, **M**easurable, **A**chievable, **R**ealistic, and **T**ime-bound. This way, you can motivate yourself to reach your end goal because they will be specifically designed in a way so that you can measure and keep track of them within a specific frame of time and space. Setting *specific* goals is important as it gives you a lot of clarity about what exactly do you need motivation for- it helps cut down on vague generalizations and compels you to define your goals in distinctly specific terms.

**Find a good momentum:** Motivation is easy to find once you have found yourself a good rhythm or momentum. Once you get going, then it is more likely that you would be on a winning streak, but initiating that, you have to establish momentum first. To set the momentum, you can try picking easier tasks to do at the beginning, which gives you a sense of accomplishment once you complete them so that it becomes easier and easier for you to transition to more complex tasks. Once you have put your finger on a good rhythm that gets you going, motivating yourself to stay on that path is not all that difficult.

**Be aware of your company:** Although it is of utmost importance to seek motivation from yourself, it is also true that it becomes hard to self-motivate if you are surrounded by people who are constantly bringing you down with constant negativity and discouragement. Surrounding yourself with people who have a positive outlook towards things is a significant step in motivating yourself, but to begin with, being aware of the sort of energy people around you exude and affect you is a good idea.

**Celebrate the smaller victories:** One of the surefire ways of keeping self-motivation intact is to celebrate the smaller victories, the insignificant ones, the ones which often go unnoticed. It is important to celebrate these victories so that you can remind yourself from time to time of the smaller steps which add to the bigger success and how indispensable these tiny victories are. Give yourself a little pat on the back, remind yourself how proud you are of your progress, and keep going at it. However, do not indulge yourself too much, or you might lose sight of the bigger picture you have been ultimately aiming for all this time.

**Use positive reinforcements:** This one is sort of an extension of the last point on this list. Positive reinforcements help you set a positive and effective pattern of behavior. For using positive reinforcements, you need to pick yourself out smaller rewards for tasks you had been sitting on for way too long, tasks that seem unattainable but can be conquered if you put your mind to it. Even if the bigger picture stops making sense at times, the momentary reward at the end of the task can act as motivation enough to get that done, and once you are on the way to finishing tougher tasks, you can incorporate it into a pattern of problem-solving to help you out in changing your behavior overall.

**Be wise about how you utilize time:** Time management is key to anything you want to achieve in life- be it a big goal or a smaller one. Utilize your time wisely by scheduling and blocking your time for specific tasks, events, and appointments. Turn certain hours of your working time into 'Do Not Disturb' periods by turning your notifications off so that you can be more present and aware during those chunks of time. Also, remember to not sign up for too many things so that your schedule is not so overburdened that you do not have enough time for leisure and other activities which are not related to work.

**Nip procrastination at the bud:** Procrastination is perhaps the biggest deal-breaker when it comes to getting something done or sometimes, even motivating yourself to get out of bud. In order to attain small and big victories, you must make sure that you are not procrastinating to the extent that you are not getting anything done at all. It is only human to delay your tasks a little bit every now and then, but do not sit on things for longer than you must. Depending on the priority, you can set a 3-minute, 3-hour, or 3-day deadline for the tasks at hand. Within that period, you must get to it. Setting this deadline also helps because often with procrastinating, we tend to keep things aside because we tell ourselves that we have all the time in the world to get to it, but once all the time' boils down to just a few hours or days, we are more likely to be pushed harder to finish the task we are consciously delaying on.

**It is smart to ask for help:** Unlike what we are often forced to believe, there is absolutely no harm in asking for help in case we are stuck. In fact, it is an absolutely smart idea to ask for some extra support when you know someone has more expertise in getting the task at hand accomplished. You will not just get your immediate problem solved, but you will also learn a valuable lesson on how to deal with the problem the next time around. Other than that, asking for help is also a good idea because it is a reminder that no matter how hard the problem seems to be, it is easy to solve for at least someone; this, in turn, serves as a motivation for you to be more self-reliant when you feel stuck.

**Focus only on the next step:** If you have 24 tasks on your to-do list, then it is obviously very difficult to get all of them checked off since it does get very overwhelming when you are dealing with a cluttered mind space. However, what helps in such a case is that you only need to focus on the next task on the list and nothing else. And once you get the next one done, you can pick the 3rd one up, then the 4th, and so on. This can be done by blocking out the entirety of the list or by creating a smaller task list that is within your immediate sight. This way, you will trick your brain into thinking that you only have one thing to get to, and it will be easier to motivate yourself for that, as well.

**Give more importance to *why* and less to *how*:** The process is meaningless if the intent is not in place. Make it a habit to give more importance to why you want to do something as opposed to how you are going to do it; often, if we are not clear with the why, our how is not clear as well, because our goals are not specific and attainable. Similarly, once we are clear about the intent, it is a lot easier to motivate ourselves with the in-between steps because we know what lies at the end of it all and what about it really is important for us.

**Do not forget to hold yourself accountable:** This is another very important step you must follow in order to remain realistic and goal-oriented. If you make a mistake (like we all do), it is the best way out to own up and hold yourself accountable instead of shifting the blame to others or deliberately ignoring it happening in the first place. It is easier to seek motivation from yourself if you are honest about your strengths and shortcomings, and holding yourself accountable also helps with this because it gives you a chance to improve on where you went wrong, which was not something you could have done on your own if you had relegated the responsibility of covering up the mistake to someone else instead. (However, while it is great to be helpful, also keep in mind that you do not have to hold yourself accountable for where others went wrong because that way, you are taking away their chance to improve themselves.)

**Figure your fears out:** If something is holding you back, you need to deconstruct it and understand what about it is actually becoming a barrier between you and your end goal. If you understand the reason behind the fear, it will also become easy to dodge it. Otherwise, you would just come up with ways of getting past the fear only once, in the current situation, and although that does work in the short term, it does not help you out much about tackling the actual shortcomings in your mindset. Instead, it lets you believe that the easy way out is to not really face your problems, which is, of course, not true.

**Cut off the daily distractions:** Switch your phone off when you are in a meeting. Block streaming sites like Netflix and Youtube when you are working on a project on your laptop. Limit your screen time on social media apps and websites. Hit 'unsubscribe' on mindless emails which are adding to the clutter in your inbox. The more daily distractions you cut off, the tighter and more worthwhile your working schedule is bound to become. Often, these are long-term changes you can make at one go, such as sorting your email out or changing some settings on your phone. These 5-minute tasks have a much longer payoff, so it is completely advisable for you to invest your time and efforts in these.

**Consume media wisely:** There are tons of self-help books, documentaries, and podcasts that are designed in a way to increase your productivity and keep yourself motivated. Pick those out and make time for them in your daily routine so that you always have some conscious media to consume, which helps you stay focused on your goals. This does not mean that you have to totally cut down on your favorite books or series, but it just means that you need to cut down perhaps 30 minutes per day from those and dedicate them towards media content that helps you stay motivated and understand your workflow in a better way (so that you can keep yourself motivated in the longer run).

**Treat failures as lessons:** This one goes without saying, but do not see failures as roadblocks that you cannot get past no matter how hard you try. No roadblock is permanent, and treating every failure as a lesson and a new starting point is very important as it often helps you gain a new perspective about the work that you are doing. Failure also helps you think more creatively and be more open to intuitive problem-solving, all of which are helpful skills. Treating failures as lessons is also a good way to motivate yourself since in case you fail and feel like there is no getting back from there, you always have stories from the past to fall back upon, which show how you have managed to dodge such roadblocks earlier and reinstall your faith in your capabilities.

**Learn how to prioritize tasks and goals:** This one is applicable to both short-term tasks and long-term goals- learn how to prioritize. Set out your tasks in a way that you are getting to the most important ones first, or at least are not forgetting about them. What often tends to happen with a packed up to-do list is that since there are too many tasks on the list, you might end up feeling very accomplished after finishing half of them, but a closer look at things will remind you how you completely forgot to get to the most crucial items since all the items on a list seem like they have equal importance. This also holds true for goals and resolutions, which are more long-term in nature. Clubbing everything together gives the impression that all of them are of the same importance and need the same amount of effort to achieve, which is not really the case. Prioritizing tasks is something that you *must* do to stay on track. You can do this by color-coding or highlighting your tasks, by setting reminders on your phone, or even by deciding that you will not pick other things up until and unless you are done with your top 3 priorities for the day.

**Remember to be kind to yourself:** And, last but not least, as we have discussed in many of our previous chapters, do not forget to treat yourself with kindness. No goal is important enough to sacrifice your mental health and peace for, and if you do not preserve your own energy, then you are going to head towards burnout which is very hard to come back from. Therefore, it is always a must to take enough breaks, allow yourself to make mistakes, be grateful for what you have done and how far you have come, and treat yourself with kindness since you are your biggest source of energy and support, at the end of the day, and there can be no better motivation than kindness.

In this chapter, we briefly went over the difference between short and long terms goals, and then we discussed different ways in which we could chart our path out regarding how to achieve these goals and how to keep ourselves motivated throughout.

# Chapter 10:

# Importance of Self-Confidence – Letting go of the Codependency

Self-confidence and codependency work together like a vicious cycle. When you do not believe in yourself enough, you turn to others for validation, for a sense of worth, and for keeping you safe. This is what is known to be the root cause for codependency, also known as pathological loneliness. This is the reason why it is also called "self-love deficit disorder" because you do not love yourself enough; you tend to seek love outwardly, which is indeed a very strenuous task. However, this gradually leads to one losing his/her connection with themselves. They lose their identity in the process, letting their relationship with a person or with a thing define them through and through. In order to be independent and be in full control of one's life, it is important to break free from this behavioral pattern. It is not at all impossible to do so, and you, too, can take control of your life.

**Why do you need Self-Confidence?**
Self-confidence, in its literal sense, is the confidence you have in yourself. It is essentially your belief in and your attitude towards your abilities, talents, strengths, intelligence, and experiences. It refers to appreciating all

the uniqueness that you have and believing that you are worthy of all the good things. It means that you accept and trust your true self. Self-confidence is a fundamental element that makes you certain of who you are, what journey you will take on in life, and what you have to offer. When you believe in yourself way more than your abilities, it results in arrogance. On the other hand, you may not believe in yourself as much as you should, which leads you to low self-esteem. Therefore, understanding what self-confidence truly means is important for you to know what you are aiming for. Something known as the Dunning-Kruger effect may also take place when you keep thinking positively blindly and set unrealistic beliefs. However, it is also important to know that often self-confidence is not only a result of your abilities but your perception of yourself, how you see and value yourself.

Let us say that by now, you have a clear idea of self-confidence is and you believe that you have what it take for you to get there, but you may question its importance. Is it worth all your time, effort, and energy? Why is it so important to develop self-confidence? Self-Confidence is linked to every element of your life involved in making it happier and fulfilled. The more self-confident you become, the more your overall life starts to improve. Here are a few reasons why you need self-confidence in your life:

**-Achieving Goals:** Self-confidence gives you the belief in the abilities that are within you. It helps you come out of your shell and realize and acknowledge the immense amount of potential within you. When you acknowledge your passion, potential, strength, and abilities, nothing can stop you from achieving your dreams, no matter how big or small they are. You will find yourself achieving your goals in contrast to when you were low on confidence and did not act up. Self-confidence gives you the push you need to take action and do so while believing in yourself and your strengths.

**-Positivity:** Self-confidence helps you in acquiring a more positive mindset. It changes your perception of who you are, what purpose you want to fulfill, and the perception of how you see others and the world. A positive mindset keeps you grateful and content rather than comparing yourself to others and desiring things one after the other, bringing in unhappiness and negativity. A negative mindset gets you nowhere. While many of you may argue that a negative perception keeps you skeptical and therefore saves you from harm, however, the truth is quite the opposite. While the negative mindset may keep you from risks but it is not keeping you safe. It is stunting your growth and never letting you go out of your comfort zone to get what you deserve. Growth and comfort do not go hand in hand. Growth gives you the freedom and takes you places, while comfort makes you a prisoner within yourself. Growth does not happen without self-confidence.

**-Independence**: Developing self-confidence brings you freedom in every aspect of your life. When you are confident, you are free of self-doubt, you start seeing your worth and the value you hold. Likewise, the more confidence you develop, the more you become capable of handling situations, relationships, outcomes, etc. You become open to learning and accepting. Once you value yourself and are confident about your abilities, you are free of judgment from yourself, and as for other people, their perception of you will no longer matter as you do not rely on their validation anymore. Confidence sets you free from anxiety and stressful thoughts; it also brings you freedom from toxic relationships with people and things.

**-Greater Success**: You may have noticed that the most successful people of our time are all very self-confident. Their confidence radiates through their work, their presence, the way they talk, the way they have tackled all obstacles to get where they are now. What do you think helped them get this far? Well, they all have one thing in common; self-confidence. Self-confidence, among many other factors, has helped them achieve their dreams because they never stopped believing in themselves, they never chose comfort over growth, they never let anyone tell them that they are not worth it. They chose to believe in their abilities, and that belief got them their dreams even when they had a life full of obstacles. You can, too; you can go out there and claim the place in the world you deserve. All you have to do is be confident in yourself, your strengths, and your abilities. Self-confidence will bring you the breakthrough you have been hoping for.

## How does confidence help you overcome codependency?

Freeing yourself from a codependent relationship is extremely important for a better life and personal development, and the foundation and the core for this achievement is to develop self-confidence. Relationships bring together two different people, completely different in ideologies, understanding, experiences, past, values, and ego. Among all these, differences arise quite inevitably, and you will need the confidence to sort through the differences and build healthier relationships. However, when you lack the confidence to face it and when you do not believe in yourself enough, you seek out the other person for help, validation, and value, which eventually results in a codependent relationship. When you lack the confidence to hold your ground, you lose your identity in the relationship. You have to make sure that your relationship is a two-way process and is based on equality and respect. You have to prioritize yourself, your ambitions, values, and goals, and none of these are truly possible without self-confidence.

## How can we prioritise self-care & increase the awareness?

Being in a codependent relationship will result in a loss of your independence. As codependents, we tend to put our needs at the very bottom of our priority list, sacrificing our independence and needs to make other people happy and to avoid conflict. While you may be doing this out of love, it is important to understand the difference between caring for someone and enabling someone. Helping someone out like children or the elderly is definitely caring as they need it; however, helping someone or taking their place when they themselves are perfectly capable is not caring for them rather enabling them till they become so dependent that you become responsible for their needs and you have no room to breathe for yourself. Self-care is not optional; it is the essence, the foundation, and the pillar of our mental and emotional wellness. Self-care for codependents is especially difficult as it comes from a place of fear and hurt; however, it is about unlearning these maladaptive coping behaviors that have developed and have taken root in you. Sel-care will empower you and help you achieve happiness and control over your own life.

Healing starts from self-care, and here are a few ways how you can prioritize self-care:

**-Permit yourself:**

It might sound unusual, but you have to give yourself the permission to start caring for yourself and enjoy the things that you value. Nothing and nobody is holding you back as much as you are, and nobody has the power or control over you except for you. Therefore, start allowing yourself to indulge in self-care, tell yourself it is extremely important. Permit yourself to take on this journey.

**-Value yourself instead of seeking validation from others:**

It is important to remember that love does not have to be worked hard for or earned. You do not have to please people so that they love you; we are all lovable and meant to be loved by the right people naturally. Love comes naturally, and we are all inherently worthy of it. Therefore, you need to value yourself more instead of relying on other people to tell you your worth. You need to realize your worth and that it is incomparable to anyone else, and nobody can define it. When you do not have enough confidence to believe in yourself and depend on other people for validation, you are giving away your power. You are letting them take control of you and your life. Therefore, have confidence, believe in yourself, and know that you are worthy and that you do not have t please other people to tell you what you always have been worthy.

**-Strong sense of self :**

As codependents, we tend to give so much to other people that they lose themselves in the process. We lose our identity in our relationship and let the relationship define us. Do not lose what is important to you while you give your important time and effort to your relationships. Developing a stronger sense of self will help you find your identity again. Try to reconnect with what you enjoy, what brings you value, and what is important to you. Reconnect and make time for those things. You need to learn to derive value and worth. from what you love doing and what makes you instead of deriving your value from being someone's partner or friend. You define your own worth.

**-Self-compassion:**

Codependents are often too harsh on themselves and are quick to judge or criticize themselves. We often set unrealistic goals and expectations, expect ourselves to be nothing short of perfect, and when we slack or fail, we beat ourselves up. Treat yourself with the same loving warmth and kindness that you treat others with.

**-Let them make their own choices:**

Understand that you are not responsible for other people. It is important because while codependents tend to acre quite too much, they may also become controlling. You are not responsible for their happiness, sadness, anger, well-being, or choices. Instead of mandating yourself into making the right choices for them when it is truly not your responsibility, let them make their own decisions and be responsible for the choice they made. Understand that you cannot control everything or everyone; the only one you can take control of is you. We cannot make someone else change or get help even when we want the best for them. Trying to force solutions and opinions only makes things worse. This will not only set you free but will also help them become more independent

**-Set boundaries**:

Setting boundaries is very important for self-care and self-preservation. It protects you when others tend to take advantage of your kindness. While many people may believe that setting up boundaries to be unkind and selfish, they truly are not. It is important for you to protect your needs and your wellness too, you mustn't let anybody manipulate you or take advantage of your kindness. Boundaries are essential to communicate what you want, how you want to be treated, what you expect, and what is not okay. It keeps you safe and helps you create safety in relationships. Therefore, it is important to set boundaries and be assertive about them.

**Seek help**:

While it may not be easy as codependents do not wish to be seen as weak and may take a liking to feel superior in the role of always being the helper, it is important for you to understand that you may not always be helping and you may not even be superior. You never know, but people may be taking advantage of your kindness and seeking help from you when they are perfectly capable, draining the life out of you. It is an unreal expectation to do everything by yourself and not need help. This may exhaust you physically and mentally; therefore, seeking help is necessary, whether it be from your family or friends or a professional.

**-Embrace solitude:**

Being able to thrive while being alone is a form of self-care. An alone time where you get to do things only for yourself and enjoy yourself in your own company is very a very liberating experience. Separating yourself from another and still being whole and complete and in control of your life is independence. Spending time with yourself will help you reconnect with yourself and your values; it will help you regain your identity as an individual and help you be happy with who you are. While codependents usually fear being alone due to past experience, giving yourself some time and space will show you that you do need anyone else to make you happy and will bring you freedom and independence.

**-Remember to be gentle:**

As codependency is a result of fear, hurt, and survival mechanisms, change may be slow-paced. Unlearning all the behavioral patterns and starting from scratch is not an easy task, but be strong and let it take time. Nothing is better rushed. Acknowledge self-awareness, be proud of yourself and honor the journey you are on. All of this is possible and accelerated by being aware and understanding yourself, your emotions, your actions, and also of others. Self-awareness will help you:

- Reflect on your actions,

- Accept and acknowledge yourself and others,

- Self-development, and

- Increased productivity.

Here is how you can increase your self-awareness:

**1- Keep a journal** - a journal will help you keep track of your emotions and actions and how you deal with them. It will show you areas where you will need to focus on and take care of.

**2- Meditate** - Meditating will help you keep your emotions in check and balance. It will help you calm down when you are erratic with your thoughts and emotions.

**3- Practice mindfulness** - Practicing mindfulness will help you perceive things better and will help you observe your thoughts and emotions in a calm, accepting, and loving manner.

**4- Personal values** - Take time to understand your values. What drives you? Why truly are you doing things the way you are doing? are they aligning with your values? Are your values right and true and not Influenced? Asking these questions to yourself now and then will bring a great deal of understanding to the surface.

# How can we empower us to step out of the victim role forever?

It is very difficult to leave victimhood behind as it comes from a very painful and traumatic place. Nobody consciously chooses to be a victim, and nobody is aware of it until they develop enough self-awareness or are confronted by someone that they realize they have been suffering from victimhood all this time. This is quite common in a codependent relationship with other people or with things as well. However, while it is difficult to empower oneself and let go of victimhood, it is not impossible. Here are a few ways for self-empowerment:

**-Take responsibility:**

Take responsibility for your choices and decisions and say "I want to" instead of "I have to." Taking responsibility helps you initiate change. It helps you make choices and accept them.

**-Take action :**

Take necessary action for your needs and your goals to be fulfilled. Instead of relying on someone else to do something for you, do it yourself. You will feel empowered and independent.

**-Do not blame:**

Do not blame others for your happiness, sadness, anger, mood, or anything. Take responsibility for your feeling and emotions. When you do, you start working for yourself; you will start doing things that will make you happy. You will have control over your life and not someone else, and that will lead to the change you want. Be responsible for yourself and your part and not for anybody else who is perfectly capable of taking responsibility for their own.

**-Be assertive :**

This will help you protect your boundaries and will empower you to not take any less than you deserve.

**-Values:**

Align yourself with your goals and values. Take control of your life and work towards achieving your goals. Remind yourself every now and then what your values are until the point they come naturally to you no matter what you do or e=what situation you are in. Being in alignment with your values will give you confidence, increase your self-esteem and help you become your authentic self.

**-Cultivate self-confidence:**

Believing in yourself and your abilities is very important. You have to emphasize this to yourself and start believing in your potential. Self-confidence is the essence of the life you desire, and it will bring you independence.

**-Seek help from your close ones or consult a professional:**

Seeking help does not make you weak or small. It will widen your horizons and open doors for new perspectives.


You may have acquired at least a small amount of knowledge and confidence to make a change for yourself and your goals. Remember that making yourself a priority and taking care of yourself first before you take care of anybody else is very important for you and your loved ones too. If you do not love yourself, how are you going to truly love another person? You have to put yourself first and acknowledge your worth so that others will too.

# Chapter 11:

# Everything you need to know about Codependency

Humans are sociable beings, and it has been that way since the beginning of time. As a result, we need other people and depend on them to survive. It is totally normal to be interdependent, it is only natural that we rely on each other, and most healthy relationships work that way. However, oftentimes, some people find it difficult not to over-indulge in a kind of behavior where they are excessively attached and giving to the other person in the relationship. When a person is not only dependent upon someone for financial, emotional, physical, psychological, and/or spiritual support but is excessively attached to this idea of support in an all-consuming manner, he/she is known to be codependent. The relationship is dysfunctional and toxic for all people involved in the relationship. Having said that, a majority of us are inclined to such behavior, whether consciously or subconsciously. It is, therefore, extremely important that we understand this behavioral and relationship pattern and learn how we can avoid it or get out of it before it is too late.

# What is codependency?

The term "codependency" and "codependent" are being used colloquially in recent times to describe close and tight relationships with varying levels of neediness, deciphering the term to mean desperation without actually knowing the true meaning and psychology behind it. Codependency is a term that is used to describe an unhealthy relationship that a person may share with their closest ones. Also known as relationship addiction, it is a psychological construct that involves an unhealthy, toxic relationship wherein a person by being excessively caring, high-functioning, and loving in an all-consuming manner not just supports the other person involved in the relationship but perpetuates them and "enables" them to continue their destructive and reckless behavior. Enabling basically means helping another person reach their end. However, in the context of codependency, it generally means enabling or helping another person to continue going down their destructive path. Codependency can be found in any relationship, be it a romantic relationship, familial relationship, or friendship. The pattern of a codependent relationship is often imbalanced wherein the partner takes up the role of a giver or rescuer, and the other person involved is in the role of a taker or a victim. These roles are assumed consciously or unconsciously; the codependent giver usually has the qualities of being an empathetic, high-functioning, and forgiving person who is extremely loving and caring, making sacrifices to provide for, emotionally, physically, financially, etc., the taker. This extreme role makes the codependent taker, who is usually addicted, troubled, under-functioning, rely on the giver for taking care of them, for covering up their shortcomings and incompetence, and to provide for them no matter what. Therefore, a codependent relationship is based on enabling the partner rather than empowering them as most healthy relationships do. However, while the person assuming the giver role may appear to be altruistic, their codependent behavioral pattern exhibits their weaknesses such as:

- Low self-esteem

- Exessive need to please others

- Decision-making problems

- Trouble identifying their emotions

- Attachment issues

- Desire to be rendered important

- Weak inter-personal boundaries

These are some of the traits that are found in common in codependents. Although all of them are natural human tendencies, it is important to understand that codependents take these traits to the extreme, and they feel it in an extreme manner. Codependency usually has a dysfunctional relationship function lying underneath, such as the partner of the codependent being an alcoholic, a substance abuser, an addict, or mental health and behavioral problems. The term "codependency" and the concept behind it first emerged in the 1950s-80s and was originally applied only to the person and their caretaking patterns of their alcoholic partner. However, it now covers a broader spectrum and not just addiction. Codependency can lead a person to lose his own identity, letting the relationship define them. They are too busy fixing others' problems that they forget to take care of themselves and lose themselves on the way. They may also feel unable to come out of this relationship after a while as they become unsure of whether their partner will be able to survive on their own. The receiving partner, on the other hand, loses a sense of responsibility, not caring about the negative consequences their actions might bring. Therefore, creating an emotional boundary or distance from the troubled or needy partner is crucial for both persons. Codependency may feel overwhelming; however, it can be overcome.

**What codependency is not?**

We, as humans, are designed to be interdependent. We need to rely on others; we need to seek help; we need our loved ones to support us and to support them in return. It is important to understand that we are not codependents when we lean on others. Codependency comes into play when we go to the extreme end of supporting or helping someone to the point where the people in the relationship start to suffer, suffocate and sacrifice their own needs. When we come across the word codependency or codependence, we immediately think of the word dependent. The term codependency can therefore be misunderstood or confused with dependence. We see dependency in everyday life, and it is not a maladaptive behavior or unusual. We all depend upon one another, and we are designed to do so. Recently, the label of codependence is overused, and the true meaning of it is misunderstood, confused, and not really known by the users.

**How is codependency related to addiction?**

Addiction to anything, be it drugs, gambling, alcohol, etc., is extremely challenging and one of the worst parts about it is how far-reaching and destructive on so many levels it can be. Moreover, unfortunately, addiction affects not only the addict but also the people around him, such as his loved ones, family members, partners, etc. Although it may not turn them into addicts too, it may gradually lead to codependency wherein the loved ones try to care for, provide for and maintain stability for the addict, consciously or unconsciously, enabling them to continue their disruptive journey. As codependency is a dysfunctional relationship, it often appears in relationships that involve addiction. Having said that, codependency does not necessarily transpire in a relationship with addiction involved; it may be seen in addiction-free relationships too; however, it is highly likely for codependency and addiction to co-occur.

In fact, codependency as a term and concept first emerged in the 1950s to describe a particular behavioral pattern in the caregiver or partners of alcoholics that would enable them.

The bond between addiction and codependency usually tends to form when the codependent starts behaving in a way that enables to addict to continue his or her addiction. Of course, nobody wants to enable someone they love and are dear to them to continue their addictive behaviors, given the self-destruction it brings about.

Most of them only try to help them, support them and care for them.

However, it is important to understand that no matter the intentions, that kind of help may not be truly helpful for an addict who you should be helping to recover than to enable them more.

You may be unconsciously enabling them, and here are a few signs you may want to watch out for if you want to know:

- Taking responsibility for the loved one without assessing if they are right or wrong

- Making excuses for their behaviors

- Covering up their lies or behavior

-Agreeing with the loved one's excuse, reason, justification for substance abuse

-Financially supporting them in substance-related problems

The problems mentioned above may not seem as bad to you, and we do all of these things to help out a loved one. However, it is important to understand that this is a situation that involves addiction. Enabling a person may give you momentary satisfaction as you may feel you are helping a loved one, but in the long run, the detrimental effects of addiction are inevitable even though your intentions are good. Shielding them will never allow them to face the negative results of their addiction and will never allow them to confront it. Therefore, you have to make sure you help them the right way.

Here are some ways how you can avoid enabling addiction:

-Avoid taking responsibility for your loved one's actions and behaviors.

-Allow your loved ones to face the results and confront the consequences of their actions and behaviors.

-Avoid taking the blame for something you have not done or if you are not wrong.

-Avoid feeling guilty when you are not wrong.

-Let your loved ones know that it is important to seek the right kind of help and urge them to do so.

Codependency and addiction can be seen to manifest in ways, such as:

-Between partners who are addicted to substance abuse

-Between a close adult addicted to substance abuse and a younger person

-Between an adult and a younger child addicted to substance abuse

The coexistence of codependency and addiction is twofold and does not only end at a person showing tendencies of codependence due to the partner being addicted to substance abuse. Codependency, also known as relation addiction, can be considered as a type of addiction wherein the person in a relationship with an addict of substance-abuse is addicted to the addict. Or, it can be an addiction to the behavioral pattern such as enabling and caretaking of the addict. It may stem from a codependent's low self-esteem and his or her constant need for validation and external levels of worth from another person. This leads to a vicious cycle of continual patterns of destructive behavior as it ensures that the addicted person never breaks away from the addiction and the codependent person, with each act of enabling their partner, becomes more and more addicted to the relationship.

A codependent may be open to such risks and effects:

1- High risk of developing an addiction along with their partner, either of substance abuse or an addiction to certain patterns and behaviors or the relationship and the partner

2- Increase in low sense of self-worth and self-esteem as a result of neglecting own personal needs for the partner

3- Inability to be responsible for anything except for the relationship and the partner

4- Loss of social life and having low chances of having a healthy relationship with other people as a result

5- Immaculate feelings of loss over an end of a relationship

6- High risk of obsessive behavioral patterns

The addicted partner may also suffer as he or she may never get to achieve recovery from the addiction due to the enabling behaviors of the codependent. Furthermore, it is possible the codependent or the enabler may intentionally never stop enabling due to fear of the loss of their partner should any change or recovery happen. The interplay between codependency and addiction causes a great deal of harm to both the people involved; hence, it is necessary to break away.

**Why is it important to find your independence again?**

Codependency can be extremely harmful as it takes a person tends to make a relationship their everything, neglecting every aspect of their own life except the relationship, even their own well-being. The desire to feel loved and to love is felt by all of us; however, when it takes an extreme form, a person becomes addicted to seeking validation from others. Codependency is a result of low self-esteem, seeking external validation, and not feeling loved. However, it is extremely important to understand that codependency does make it right or bring an end to these thoughts and emotions, but rather codependency ensures it stays that way or even worse. You lose more of your self-esteem depending upon another person to tell you your worth; you go to the extreme of sacrificing your own needs in order to please another person, in order to be validated by another person, in order to feel worthy and loved. You try to please them more and more, wanting more of the affection and the validation. However, in the middle of all that, you lose yourself, your identity, your goals, your dreams, and your ambitions. One of the most detrimental effects of codependency is losing one's identity. You become so addicted to the relationship that you start letting yourself be defined by your relationship. Your identity and your individuality are lost trying to hold your relationship. A majority of codependents do not succeed in life because they let a relationship consume themselves that they forget to prioritize themselves and their future. They often end up lost and bitter.

Your sense of low self-worth and your loss of identity only deepens in codependency.

The long-term effects of codependency are as follows:

-Disempowered

-Fearful

-Feeling unsafe

-Low self-esteem

-Loneliness

-Depressed and anxiety

-Identity crisis

-Disconnected from yourself, from others, and reality

-Trust Issues

-Unsuccessful

-Shame

Therefore, it is extremely important that you break free from its shackles and reclaim your life as your own and start prioritizing yourself over everybody else and see your life transform.

**How to understand, accept & break free from the codependent cycle?**

When a person is unknowingly codependent, it is quite difficult to understand the patterns as most of it passes or is often ignored for normal human behavior of wanting to be loved and accepted. Certain behavior patterns do not seem to a sign of codependence, at least not at first. However, these behaviors start becoming extreme with time. Here are some of the signs that will help you understand codependency and if your behavioral patterns do match:

- A desperate need to please others

- Constant worrying and feeling anxious

- Fear of rejection

- Fear of abandonment

- Low self-esteem

- Not being able to identify one's own feelings

- Not being able to trust one's own instincts and feelings

- Staying in bad relationships and sabotaging good ones

- Feeling depressed and isolated

- Taking extreme measures to take care of others

- Feeling guilty for not being good enough

- Difficulty communicating your thoughts and emotions

- Intense emotional reactions

- Need for control

- Obsessing over other people

- Familial dysfunction

- Poor emotional boundaries

Codependency may seem overwhelming. However, healing is possible. No matter how difficult it may seem, it is upon you to make a choice to transform your life free of the emotional restraints that affect every single aspect of your life. Healing is possible if you make a choice. Once you have made a choice, you have already made up your mind; nothing can stop you as long as you are determined to not fall back to the same vicious cycle again, now or in the future.

The first step to healing is acceptance. Acceptance will set you free; you will not have to lie to yourself anymore. Accepting your emotions, feelings, thoughts, and needs is the first step. Accept yourself the way you are, accept your emotions that you have been keeping at bay, accept your feelings even if they are bad, accept your needs and understand and accept the relation you have with codependence. Acknowledge them, deal with them - dealing with all these things that you have kept afar may be difficult at first, but once you start, you will realize how free you are becoming. When you acknowledge yourself and your feeling, emotional needs, you do not need any acknowledgment from others. Acceptance and acknowledgment is the first step towards breaking free and healing from codependence. As already mentioned, it is extremely important to break free from codependence. And while it may take some time, it is never impossible. Here are a few tips on how you can break free:

**-Get in tune with your needs:**

Sometimes, we may put some of our needs aside to help someone; however, throwing away all our needs in order to please someone is not compassion or selflessness. Prioritize your needs, write them down, ask yourself what do *you* need? Reconnect with all of your passions and priorities. Figure out what you truly need in life and chase it. When you know what your needs are, it will be difficult to shake them off, hence, reminding you to focus on your needs time and again.

**Self-awareness:**

Breaking out of codependency starts from self-awareness. You need to recognize your own codependent behaviors and tendencies. Being mindful of your own tendencies will not only help you get out of a codependent relationship if you are in one but will also stop you from falling into a pitfall of one more codependent relationship in the future. Keep a journal and pen down your thoughts and feelings, and observations; it will help you to have a clear line of thoughts.

**Create firm boundaries:**

As you may already know by now, codependent people often have a difficult time setting boundaries with other people. This prompts other people to take advantage of your kindness and your willingness to give. Saying no or putting your needs first, or stopping other people from shoving their problems and troubles towards you may be difficult, but it is extremely rewarding. Setting up a boundary and being assertive about it will provide you your own space where you will not have to deal with any of other people's troubles, and it is extremely important for peace of mind and to align with your emotions and priorities. Setting up boundaries will bring you freedom.

**Stop feeling powerless and take action:**

Codependent individuals often deal with a deep-seated fear and depend upon other people to empower them. However, no one can replicate or take away the power within you that you just have to take control of. You can empower yourself, and it won't happen unless you step out and take control of your life.

**-Embrace being alone:**

Stop fearing being alone and embrace it whenever you get the chance to be alone with yourself. Learn about yourself, Delve deeper into your feelings, pamper yourself, take care of yourself, treat it like it is a special time just for you because it is. Let go of codependency and start by making a small change today for a bigger brighter tomorrow.

# Chapter 12:

# A guide to forming healthy relationships

Humans are inherently social beings, and we seek to form connections with other people. This sums up our primary drives, along with that of food and shelter. Relationships play a major role in healthy and successful living, and they enrich our lives. However, connecting with someone and sharing love and respect is not a privilege available to everyone. Every relationship, irrespective of the type, be it a friendship, a romantic relationship, work relationship, or a familial relationship, has its ups and downs, which are in fact significant. However, some relationships may start off on a very unhealthy or toxic foundation or may get there as the relationship progresses. One such example would be a codependent relationship, also known as relationship addiction, wherein the partner is unhealthily attached to the other person who, in return, in most cases, suffers from an addiction. The partner is, therefore, said to be codependent and does everything in his or her capability to support the other person so that he or she is valued, needed, loved, and deemed worthy as a codependent person himself or herself suffers from low self-esteem and seeks validation from another person. However, in playing the role of the rescuer, the provider, and the giver, the partner is not truly empowering the other person but enabling them to continue their disruptive and unhealthy behaviors and addiction. Also, the partner or the codependent does not gain anything but loses more of what is left of himself or herself, with low self-esteem becoming lower and not being able to identify himself or herself out of the relationship. This is only one of the examples of how unhealthy relationships can form and the detrimental effects they can have on the people who are involved in such a relationship. This makes it all the more important that we form healthy relationships.

**What is a healthy relationship?**

A healthy relationship is one that is filled with happiness, enjoyment, love, respect, support, empowerment but most importantly, room for growth, personal freedom, and independent individual identities. At the same time, it is also important to remember that there is no static definition of a healthy relationship because it differs from person to person and is subjective to different opinions, goals, and experiences. Furthermore, it is also ever-evolving; you do not remain the same person throughout your life, and therefore, your idea of a healthy relationship also changes accordingly as a result of a change in your priorities, your age, your perspective, goals, and so on but the basics and the founding pillars still remain the same; it must remain the same. Having said that, it is important to understand that relationships are not meant to be flawless and perfect. There will be challenges along the way with inevitable frustration and fights; that is what makes a relationship strong. Minor fights, arguments, and opposing opinions are bound to occur because it is two different identities, personalities, opinions, dreams, past experiences, and ego coming together.

However, take any of it to the extreme, and the relationship will become unhealthy. When arguments do not come to an end, when fights escalate into violence and when a person in the relationship starts to suffer, feel suffocated, and entrapped inside the relationship, that is already a warning bell of an unhealthy and toxic relationship.

A healthy relationship is not always the case because we often end up allowing the wrong people into our lives, or we become the wrong person for someone else, and our relationship with them does not spur any positive, successful, and fruitful outcome.

## What makes a healthy relationship?

Every person in the world is unique with their own set of unique ideas, visions, and experiences, and therefore every relationship is unique. A relationship is said to be healthy when the people involved in it share the same end they want out of the relationship. Every relationship has a difference in degree but not in kind.

The basic foundations of a healthy relationship remain the same even though they are unique to every person and no matter what goals and ends they want the relationship to provide.

Understanding these basic founding pillars of a healthy relationship will help you to form and enjoy a relationship that is fulfilling and empowering.

Here are the basic principles:

# -Purpose:

Whenever you are starting a new relationship, you should keep in mind what you want and how you want the relationship to align with our needs, our goals, and our vision, and also if you are ready to align with the other person's wants and needs too. Having a sense of purpose when you get into a relationship is not selfish as traditionally implied; rather, it helps the relationship bloom into a beautiful and healthy one. It is extremely important as it has now been backed by research and studies that most who get into a romantic relationship end up living together and even marrying even though one of them or even both had agreed that they were not right for each other at the beginning. This may happen due to the thought of having spent a lot of time together that they feel they have to go through with the relationship no matter how it is getting in their way or is not aligning with their own lives. Researchers from the University of Denver in Colorado have reported that "Many, if not most, couples slide from non-cohabitation to cohabitation before fully realizing what is happening; it is often a non-deliberative and incremental process." Therefore, the phrase "Start as you go" implies relationships as well.

**-Personal boundaries and limits:**

When someone or something threatens your well-being, you limit their access to you, right? In the same way, it is important for you to have your boundaries and protect your emotional harmony and well-being even in a relationship. You need to make sure that you are safe, your emotions are safe, and that you do not have to give up everything for another person to value you and love you. Likewise, it is your responsibility that you limit yourself from invading another person's boundaries. They are there for a reason, and if the relationship is in alignment and equal harmony, then eventually these walls will come down on their own without threat, but it is important to not force it. The concepts of "Healthy Closeness" and "Healthy Distance" play a very important role in a relationship, be it of any kind. If your relationship is invading your boundaries despite your unwillingness, it is time for you to take a step back and re-evaluate things with a calm mind and make a decision. Boundaries should be respected.

**Open communication:**

Communication is the key in any relationship and the failure of which sabotages the relationship. You should be comfortable in communicating things that are going on in your life, things you want to pursue, or even small things. You should also be able to communicate your feelings and emotions to them and as time goes by you should be able to communicate some serious matters too. However, communication, like any other element in the relationship, should be reciprocated.

The other person should also be able to and be comfortable communicate with you just as you are. Communication is one of the most important elements because think about it; if you don't talk, how are you going to maintain the relationship anyway?

Therefore, you should always communicate, and if you cannot or are not comfortable, then it may be a sign.

**Conflict resolution:**

Communication is also very important to resolve a conflict in a relationship because conflicts will naturally arise from time to time. It is only natural that conflicts arise now and then, and you feel frustrated and so on, but it does not mean that the relationship is unhealthy. What makes a difference is how you respond to it and whether you are willing to resolve it or not. Unresolved conflict will bring the relationship deeper into a struggle and will cause you to stress, become anxious, feel sad, and will affect your activities; therefore, it is important that conflicts do not become an end but an obstacle for the people involved in a relationship to resolve together and forgive each other. There should not be any judgment, contempt, or grudge to hold on to in a healthy relationship. It is also important to remember that conflict should not take the form of violence of any kind.

**Individuality:**

A healthy relationship is one where you do not lose yourself and start getting defined by your relationship. A relationship is the coming together of different people,

and therefore a healthy relationship should allow you to pursue your hobbies and passions and have a social life outside of the relationship. A healthy relationship is an interdependence. It means that you do depend and rely on each other for mutual support, help, and understanding but not to the point where you cannot take care of your own needs. You are a unique individual, and you should be able to maintain your identity and individuality even when you are interdependent in your relationship. A balance in a relationship should always be maintained. Even though you share mutual love and support but that does not mean your self-esteem should also come from your relationship.

**Trust:**

Every person in a relationship should be able to have confidence in one another. You should be confident that they will not do things to offend you or lie to you when you are away or behind your back and vice versa. However, trust does not only mean cheating on you or lying to you. You should be able to confide in them, trust them that they will not hurt you, physically or emotionally, that they have your best interests in their mind and will always support you, advise you but will also trust you enough to make your own decisions and respect those decisions.

**Respect:**

Love is not the only thing that sustains a relationship of any kind. It is sustained by mutual respect. You should have mutual respect for each other, one another's dreams, passions, experiences, opinions, ideas, and decisions. You should be respectful of their boundaries and should expect the same—a relationship s successful and lasting when respect prevails, but it ends with the end of respect.

**Time apart:**

Most people have the misconception that you have to spend as much time as you can with the other person to maintain the relationship. However, it is not so. Time apart from each other every now and then is what constitutes a healthy relationship. This ensures that you do not overindulge in the relationship, or become obsessed with a person, or become codependent. Time apart allows you to spend time on yourself, invest in yourself, take care of yourself and do what you like, and feel most comfortable with yourself. You may visit your friends, family and so on or simply catch up with work. It is important to have space and time for yourself outside of any relationship.

**Sense of self-worth:**

Having a sense of self-worth means that you do not let your worth be measured or validated by your relationship or your partner. You should have enough self-esteem that you do not expect it to come to you from your relationship or your partner. A healthy relationship is one where you do not allow your partner to define your value and vice versa. This will make you lose your identity, and when you allow this to happen, you are allowing toxicity into your relationship.

**Appreciation:**

A healthy relationship is one wherein you do not take the relationship or the other person for granted. It is shown in reports all over the world that long-term relationships come to an end because their partners are not as attentive and appreciative as they were before. It is important that you give your partner and their needs attention and be appreciative of them. You should also feel the same in return.

**Intimacy:**

Upon hearing the word intimacy, people often refer to it as sex. However, intimacy not only means that but also means emotional intimacy and whether or not you are comfortable sharing physical and emotional intimacy in a relationship, especially a romantic one. Intimacy also leads to consent. A healthy relationship should be based on mutual consent and should be mutually respected. Anything in the relationship should not have to be forced upon.

**Involvement of both people:**

Forming and maintaining a relationship is teamwork. Even when you are not on the same page, when you support, empower, and love each other, you are in a healthy relationship and are a team. A relationship cannot and is not meant to be formed and maintained by a single person. A relationship has to have the commitment and the desire of all the people involved in it. Each person should be able to help each other and also have a sense of self which results in a healthy and harmonious relationship.

These are the basic principles of having a healthy relationship, and partners who address all these as a team will definitely go a long way of fulfillment and happiness.

**Why are healthy relationships so important?**
The relationships we form with other people are very important for our mental and physical well-being and for our overall survival. Relationships shape our lives right from childhood into youth to old age. It is vital for survival, and it shapes our future relationships, our ambitions, our opinions, and our perspective of life and ourselves. Healthy relationships are also vital for our health as it has been proven that it leads to a healthier, happier and longer life. On the contrary, being alone and isolated has the same effects on your health as smoking cigarettes, blood pressure, and obesity. It can also greatly impact your mental health, which can make you prone to stress, depression, and other illnesses, which then give birth to physical ailments and health issues. Arthur Aron, a psychology professor and director of the Interpersonal Relationships Laboratory at New York's stony Brooks University, says that "Relationships are - not surprisingly - enormously important for health and there are lots of studies on the biological processes that account for the

link between relationships and health." A hefty number of studies show that relationships are important for well-being.

Here are a few of the many benefits and the importance of healthy relationships:

**-Better healing:**

Healthier relationships result in faster healings from anything, be it a physical or an emotional issue. Whether it is having someone to remind you to have your medicine or someone to listen to you and be there to take care of you, studies have shown that people with healthier relationships have a greater survival and healing rate.

**-Longer life:**

Studies such as Dan Buettner's Blue Zones research calculates that committing to a life partner can add as much as three years to life expectancy.

Similarly, a review of 148 studies put to light that people who have strong social relations are 50% less likely to die prematurely.

Research shows that the lack of having a social relationship accounts for as much as smoking 15 cigarettes a day.

**-Healthier behaviors:**

Healthy relationships set the tone for a healthy lifestyle.

When you surround yourself with people who empower you instead of enabling you, you find yourself indulging in things that are good for you.

When you surround yourself with healthy people, you find yourself indulging in healthier habits and behaviors as they become a healthy influence on you and your life.

**-Less stress:**

When a person has healthy relations, he or she is more likely to deal with less stress, and even when they are in stressful situations, the emotional and physical support they get from these relationships decreases their stress levels. People who go through strenuous situations face lesser levels of stress when they are reminded of the people they share healthy relationships with. However, people who have unhealthy relationships go through more stress when they are reminded of these relations. Studies prove that healthy relationships decrease the production of cortisol, the stress hormone.

**-A greater sense of purpose:**

It is only human and natural to want to feel needed for the desire to be loved and love someone in return. Having healthy relationships allows you to do so and hence, increases your sense of self-worth, your well-being and gives you purpose in life. It helps you to empower someone, to be able to do something for someone hence, giving increasing your sense of purpose. Also, a greater sense of purpose adds to your life expectancy too.

**-Wealthier:**

Having healthy relationships is equivalent to having wealth as you are always surrounded by people who love and support you through everything in life. A survey by the National Bureau of Economic Research of 5000 people found that doubling your group of friends is equal to a 50% increase in your income and has the same effect on you and your well-being. On the contrary, unhealthy relationships, loneliness, and low social support are linked to several health issues such as :

- Depression

- Higher Blood Pressure

- Low Immune Function

Healthy relationships are important for you in every aspect of your life, and they can determine how you will go on in life. It also plays a major role in every aspect of your life. Negative relationships bring you emotional and physical turmoil and can put you in a dark place where you lose your sense of self and identity. Every individual is unique and has their own way of marching forward in life and looking after their well-being, and determining what they want from a relationship. Some people prefer being alone most of the time, and that is completely okay as wanting to be alone is not lonely. However, we need at least one relationship in our lives, and even if it is just one or a few, we need them to be healthy as it ensures experiencing genuine love, happiness, and forgiveness, and it helps us detach ourselves from harmful behaviors of others.

# Conclusion

Thank you for making it through to the end of *Self-Compassion Workbook*, let's hope it was informative and able to provide you with all of the tools you need to achieve your goals, whatever they may be. We have all heard of the advice that we must show compassion towards others, but we fail to understand that there is not much difference between self-compassion and showing compassion to others and that both these things are equally important. If you have reached this page, it means that you have already gone through the rest of the chapters, and if you have followed the tips mentioned there, then you will start seeing changes in a few weeks. You will start becoming more understanding towards yourself. Self-compassion means that you will no longer ignore your pain and show yourself the same warmth that you show to others. You will slowly start to understand that life entails various obstacles and difficulties, and you cannot stop that from happening. But what you can do is treat yourself with kindness. It is okay to be imperfect.

You won't always be or get what you want but giving in to self-criticism is not the solution.

You will also learn that your feelings should not be overexaggerated, and neither should they be suppressed. You will learn to strike a balance between both. You will learn to put everything in a larger perspective through mindfulness. You can experience emotional equanimity only when you understand the importance of kindness and show yourself sympathy. I hope that you have learned the ways in which you can practice self-compassion in your daily life, and now it is time that you start applying them whenever you can. With self-compassion, you will not only be able to achieve a greater sense of emotional stability but also better health. With practice, your sense of self-compassion will grow, and you will be able to easily defuse negativity, depression, and anxiety. If you want to free yourself from the toxic chains of frustration and self-criticism, I urge you to start taking small steps today, and you will be experiencing the benefits firsthand!

If you found this book useful in any way and if you would like to let me know your feedback on Amazon... it's always appreciated !

https://www.amazon.com/Self-Compassion-Workbook-accept-yourself-ebook/dp/B08XMFBXK7

### GET THE AUDIOBOOK VERSION
of "Self Compassion Workbook"
**FOR FREE WITH A 30 DAY AUDIBLE TRIAL**

Following this link for USA :

https://www.audible.com/pd/B0933NFF4M/?source_code=AUDFPWS0223189MWT-BK-ACX0-252040&ref=acx_bty_BK_ACX0_252040_rh_us

Following this link for UK:

https://www.audible.co.uk/pd/B0934M3D9G/?source_code=AUKFrDIWS02231890H6-BK-ACX0-252040&ref=acx_bty_BK_ACX0_252040_rh_uk

Sadie Quail

Made in the USA
Monee, IL
19 May 2021